The Second World War

Also available:

Literacy Through History series

Victorians
Ian Roberts and Brian Moses
1-84312-180-8

Britain in the 1960s and 1970s
Ian Roberts and Brian Moses
1-84312-182-4

Location Writing:
Taking Literacy into the Environment
Caroline Davey and Brian Moses
1-84312-045-3

Creative History Activity Packs

Tudors
Jane Bower
1-85346-861-4

Victorians
Jane Bower
1-85346-875-4

Ancient Egyptians
Jane Bower
1-85346-940-8

Vikings
Jane Bower
1-85346-942-4

Ancient Greeks
Jane Bower
1-85346-944-0

The Second World War

**Ian Roberts and
Brian Moses**

 **David Fulton** Publishers

David Fulton Publishers Ltd
The Chiswick Centre, 414 Chiswick High Road, London W4 5TF

www.fultonpublishers.co.uk

First published in Great Britain in 2005 by David Fulton Publishers

10 9 8 7 6 5 4 3 2 1

David Fulton Publishers is a division of Granada Learning, part of ITV plc.

Note: The right of Ian Roberts and Brian Moses to be identified as the authors of their work has been asserted by them in accordance with the Copyright, Designs and Patents Act 1988.

British Library Cataloguing in Publication Data
A catalogue record for this book is available from the British Library.

ISBN 1-84312-181-6

Designed and typeset by Kenneth Burnley, Wirral, Cheshire
Printed and bound in Great Britain

Contents

Introduction

A common concern expressed by primary school teachers is that pressure exerted on curriculum time by factors such as the National Literacy Strategy (NLS), National Numeracy Strategy (NNS) and discrete subject teaching has had a detrimental effect on creativity and enjoyment.

Word and sentence level tasks have tended to swamp opportunities for longer pieces of creative writing. Furthermore, subjects taught in isolation have resulted in lost opportunities for primary schoolchildren to appreciate links between them.

In the DFE publication *Excellence and Enjoyment*, some of these problems appear to be acknowledged. Schools are reminded that NLS materials can be adapted to meet the individual needs of schools and that the schemes published by the Qualifications and Curriculum Authority (QCA) are optional. A further crucial reminder is also given as follows:

> There is no requirement for subjects to be taught discretely – they can be grouped or taught through projects. If strong enough links are created between subjects, pupils' knowledge and skills can be used across the curriculum.

The aim of this book is to provide stimulating historical source material linked to enjoyable, purposeful and challenging language activities aimed primarily for children in Key Stage 2 of the National Curriculum.

Resources have been chosen to fulfil two requirements:

1. For their diversity and interest in relation to the historical theme being studied.

2. To encourage creative responses that allow the development and application of literacy skills.

Connections too, can be made between past and present – linking what we know now with what we find out about the past, linking who we are now and how we live today with the thoughts and deeds of our ancestors. It is about searching for clues and making comparisons between what was and what is now. It is empathising with the children who were evacuated and wondering how we would have coped in their situation. It is discovering what was eaten in times of food shortages and wondering whether we would cope with similar privations.

The photocopiable source material and suggested activities provide rich and varied opportunities to write in a wide range of genres. In addition, they present opportunities for speaking and listening, activities involving drama and further creative work. The suggested tasks can be used flexibly according to individual circumstances and specific needs of children.

Examples of usage include:

*   Shared writing tasks with the teacher modelling a particular genre within the literacy hour.

*   As additional tasks for more sustained writing outside the literacy hour.

*   Tasks for small-group work. Children can list important facts or issues and present findings to the class. A 'panel of experts' could research an area of source materials. The rest of the class could draw up a list of twenty questions that could be put to the panel.

*   Tasks for independent writing, the outcomes of which could be used for formative and summative assessment purposes.

*   Exploration of different genres: diary entries could be rewritten as news reports or letters.

- Tasks aimed at challenging talented and more able pupils by providing greater breadth and depth of learning through the provision of a wider variety of opportunities.

- Homework activities.

- As supplementary material to extend children's learning beyond the National Curriculum programmes of study.

Much of the source material comes from newspapers and magazines published during the war along with both written and illustrative material from government campaigns and extracts from school log books.

The sources provide opportunities for children to view material that was first seen by people in the Second World War. They have been chosen to develop children's interest in, and understanding of, aspects of life in Britain during that war, including evacuation, education, rationing, safety, news reporting, advertising, employment, social expectations, and domestic life.

Organisation

This book contains two main sections.

The first contains photocopiable source materials. Each source document is accompanied by short background notes and suggested activities.

In most cases, it is envisaged that teachers will introduce children to the source materials and provide opportunities for discussion of the suggested activities. An alternative approach might be to challenge more able children to work with the materials independently.

The second section of the book provides a collection of further source materials that can be used to support activities devised by teachers and pupils.

Part I

Source materials and activities

Evacuee children (1)

◄ ◉ ►

Stimulus material

Pictures of evacuee children and school log book entries 1939.

Background

Thousands of children considered to be living in areas at risk from heavy bombing were evacuated to the countryside. For many children, it was the first time that they had been away from their parents and their homes.

When the evacuees arrived in the reception areas, they were allocated to local homes and enrolled in village schools.

While some evacuee children settled into their new lives and made friends with local children, others found the changes difficult to deal with. Some city children had never seen farm animals before and were consequently frightened of them.

Sometimes it was necessary for evacuees to be re-evacuated as bombing strategy changed or the risk of invasion increased.

Suggested activities

Imagine that you are a teacher of evacuee children. Write contrasting reports on two of them. One should be about a child who has adapted well to the changes while the other report should focus on a child who has found the move extremely difficult. Your report could comment on each child's ability to make friends, respond to lessons and settle into village life.

Imagine that you are either an evacuee city child or a village child who makes friends with a child from a different area. You are then separated by re-evacuation. Write a letter to your friend. You could give news about your school and neighbourhood in addition to telling your friend about the ways in which you miss them. Remember to ask some questions in your letter. This should encourage your friend to reply!

Autumn Term   1939

Sept. 19ᵗ   School re-opened this morning with the addition of
              60 children evacuated under the Government Scheme.

May 27ʳ·   Acting on instructions from the Director, the
              evacuees have been merged into the Village School.
              Four mixed classes have been formed namely
                  Infants   under   Mrs Marton
                  Stds I · II   " "   Miss Walsh
                    " III · IV   " "   the Head Teacher
                    " V - VII   " "   Mr. Gutteridge.

      24ᵗʰ.   The evacuees having been re-evacuated to
              Wales yesterday, Guestling School now returns
              to normal routine.

July 2ⁿᵈ.   The School Garden cultivated by the evacuees has
              been left in charge of Guestling School until
              the crop has been lifted. The T.T. for the
              time being is necessarily disorganised at times to do this.
              This afternoon Std V. in charge of the Head Teacher
              went to dig potatoes, gather peas etc from
              2·40 - 3·40 . Mrs Marton was left in charge
              of the remaining Junior children for that period.

Evacuee children (2)

▬ ◉ ▬

Stimulus material

Postcard from an evacuee and quotes from accounts of evacuation plus 'The End of Evacuation' (see Section 2, p. 56).

Background

Parents were not informed as to where their children were being taken. However, on arrival, each child was issued with a postcard on which was to be written a brief message along with his/her new postal address.

Suggested activities

Attempt to empathise with what children went through: imagine coming to school with your suitcase, sandwiches and gas mask, then walking to the railway station wearing a label with your name and address written on it. Imagine boarding a train with many other children and travelling for hours and hours, stopping and starting again and again until you finally reach your destination where you are taken to some village hall and handed over to strangers, or worse still, made to stand in a bunch while the strangers pick you out one by one.

Write a postcard home which tells your parents where you are and how you are, who you are staying with, what the house is like. Are there pets?

The postcards would have been read by your foster parents so you wouldn't be able to say that you disliked your new home or were feeling homesick. But maybe you can say something in the postcard that would reveal to your parents that you weren't totally happy in your new situation.

Pamela Buckley writes of missing the things she had to leave behind. What would you miss in that situation? Who would you miss – family, pets, neighbours, friends? Make a list and offer reasons why. Would there be some things (or even people) that you wouldn't miss?

'I remember getting very upset because I had to go away from Mum and Dad and my brothers and sisters and be on my own. I had never been away from them before and it was scary.'

Ricky Clitheroe

'At that tender age it was the toys we had to leave that hurt the most. I took just one doll.'

Pamela Buckley
(Jersey)

'Although I was not the first to be picked, I was not the last. It is something I have often thought about over the years. What would it have felt like to be the one left standing alone . . .'

Ben Wicks

'Dear Mum. I hope you are well. I don't like the man's face much. Perhaps it will look better in daylight. I like the dog's face best.'

Evacuee's first postcard home

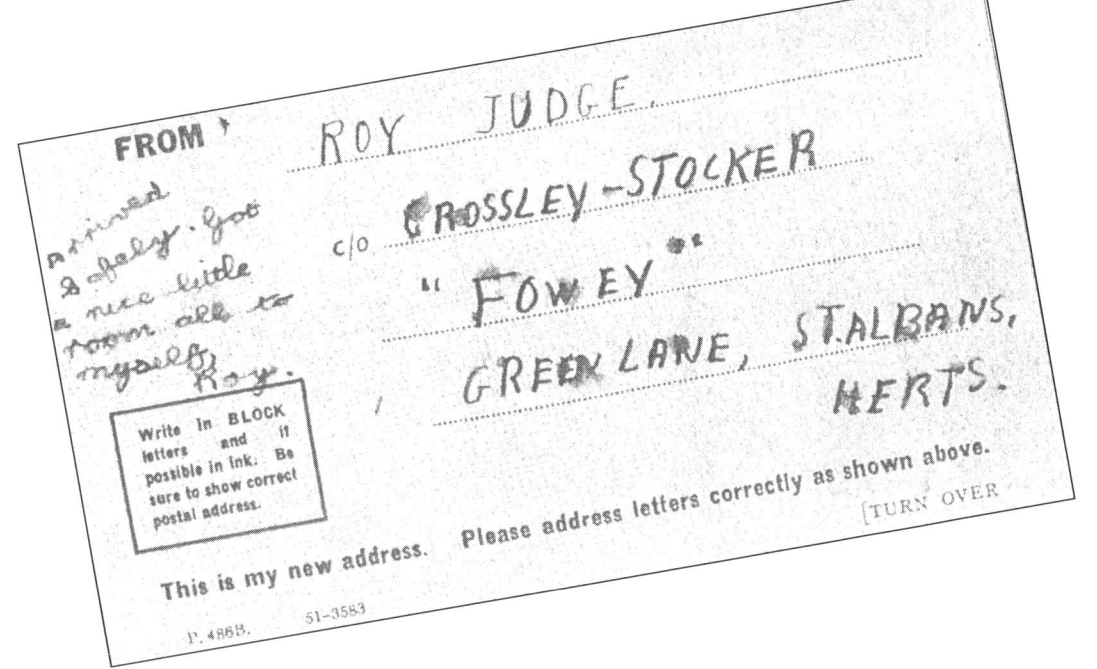

FROM ROY JUDGE.

c/o CROSSLEY-STOCKER

" FOWEY "

GREEN LANE, ST ALBANS, HERTS.

arrived safely. got a nice little room all to myself.
Roy.

Write In BLOCK letters and if possible in ink. Be sure to show correct postal address.

This is my new address. Please address letters correctly as shown above.

[TURN OVER

P. 4868. 51-3583

Evacuee children (3)

— ◉ ▸

Stimulus material

Pictures of evacuee children and posters encouraging evacuation.

Background

At the beginning of the war there was a period when there did not appear to be an immediate threat from bombing. This became known as 'The Phoney War'. Some parents were keen for evacuee children to return home.

In an effort to discourage children from returning to areas at risk from bombing, the government mounted a publicity campaign.

Suggested activity

Write a government leaflet designed to encourage evacuation and discourage the return of evacuees. Your leaflet might try to persuade parents that their children will be happy, healthy and safe in the countryside or it could emphasise the risks associated with a return to the city streets.

LEAVE THIS TO US SONNY — <u>YOU</u> OUGHT TO BE OUT OF LONDON

MINISTRY OF HEALTH EVACUATION SCHEME

MOTHERS
Send them out of London

Everyday life in wartime

Stimulus material

Newspaper articles and 'The End of Evacuation' (Section 2, p. 56).

Background

Most city schools were closed once children and teachers were evacuated. As children began to return to the cities, ways had to be found to try to educate them, and the newspaper report from Sheffield is an example of one city's attempts to continue children's school work.

Suggested activities

Discuss in groups and then list the advantages and disadvantages of the home system. Some of these can be found in the newspaper report, others will be less obvious. Would anyone prefer this system to a normal school day?

Read the newspaper report 'Lonely, Left in London' and the account 'The End of Evacuation' (p. 56). These represent two contrasting viewpoints. Archie in the report is lonely and longing to leave London, whereas the boy in the account is homesick and would do anything to get back to London.

Who do you think you would have been in this situation?

With a partner, prepare interview questions to put to either Archie or the homesick boy – you could give him a name. Either act out the interview or write up a more detailed newspaper report based on answers that have been given to your questions.

Include both boys in the same piece and, if possible, make comparisons between their answers.

Example: 'Archie told me that he really wanted to be with his mates. He'd heard from one of them and they were climbing trees and building camps. Joe (the homesick boy) told us that none of that really interested him and that it was little comfort to him if he was away from his family.'

LONELY, LEFT IN LONDON

By RITCHIE CALDER

ARCHIE APPELBY was feeling sorry for himself. He hung disconsolately over the parapet of London Bridge, gazing down on the traffic in the Pool, when I spoke to him.

Archie is not quite 13, and he is one of the thousands of school-children left behind in London when the others were evacuated.

"Why didn't you go with the rest?" I asked him.

"I wanted to," he said, with a choke in his voice. "But when they broadcast about the evacuation Dad and Mum and me were on holiday. They said 'not to rush back, but stay where we were.' And we did.

"Now all the billets from my school are filled and I can't get away until the next lot goes. Maybe I won't get with my chums after all. . . ."

Archie is one of the 8,000 London County Council children registered for the second evacuation, but awaiting Government orders.

I discussed these cases with the L.C.C. Education Department. Obviously, the 8,000 who have registered are only a few of the schoolchildren still left in London.

Only a census can discover the numbers that remain, and a census may be undertaken.

Thousands of children are roaming the streets with nothing to do, and no decision has been taken about remaining.

(*Daily Herald*, 20 September 1939)

The need for shelters

---⊙---

Stimulus material

Extracts from school log book 1940.

Background

These extracts from a school log book show that air raid shelters were not always provided. During raids, children and their teachers took shelter wherever they could. When air raids became more frequent, some parents refused to send their children to school.

Suggested activity

Imagine that you are the parent of a child who attends a school that does not have air raid shelters. Write a letter to the County Architect or the local newspaper complaining about the lack of shelters. Use the events recorded in the log book to compile a persuasive argument to encourage the provision of shelters.

1940

May 14th During the morning we rehearsed dispersing as
in the event of an air raid. Under trees
by a high hedge in an allotment was
found to be a suitable place. Mrs J. Fellows
who rents the allotment indicated has
given her permission for us to use it.

15. A.R.P. rehearsal during the morning.

17th Mr. Gooding carried out an inspection of
the children's gas masks this morning.

Aug. 2nd. A representative from the County Architect's Office
1940 called to advise on A.R.P. and the School.
He decided to recommend the small room as the
most suitable air-raid Shelter. A suggestion
that the Infants occupy that room permanently
was approved.

Aug. 5th. Air Raid Sirens sounded at approx. 2.50 p.m. Infants were already installed in the small room. Juniors immediately took up positions with them around the walls. The All-clear signal sounded at approx. 3.15 p.m. The interval was taken up with singing. The behaviour of the children was excellent.

Oct. 1st. A delayed action bomb, dropped in the night, exploded in the field opposite the school. Children immediately took cover underneath their tables & behaved well. No official intimation or warning of this had been given to the Head Teacher by the police. The caretaker had passed on the information that the bomb was there so that the children might be warned. No damage to the school was sustained.

1940

The report from the School Attendance Officer showed that the following children are not attending school because of the air raids and the fact that there is no shelter provided.

Oct. 7th
John, Betty, and Mary Oliver
Jean and John Ballard
Derek Ballard.
Joyce Bourne.
Kenneth Toth.

Oct. 9th Attendance 13 (33%). At 10.45 a.m. without warning bombs were dropped in the neighbourhood. Children took shelter under their tables.
At 11.15 a.m. an air raid warning sounded.
At 12 noon bombs dropped in immediate neighbourhood. Again children took shelter under their tables.
All clear sounded at 1.40 p.m.
Attendance this afternoon 11.
Warning at 2.45. All clear 4.20.

Wireless lessons

Stimulus material

School log book, February 1944.

Background

On 16 February 1944, the head teacher of a school reports the 'unexpected delivery of a wireless' (radio).
On 26 February 'Wireless lessons' began. The infant children listened to a twenty-minute broadcast called 'Let's Join In'.

Suggested activities

Imagine that you are a member of the production team on 'Lets Join In'. What would you include in your broadcast? You might, for example, include a short story, poems, songs and information. Plan and produce your broadcast. You could record your work and play it to younger children.

Extension activity

Plan and produce a broadcast for older children on the theme of 'Stories From History'.

Feb 1944

16ᵗʰ A wireless set having been installed quite unexpectedly the necessary arrangements have not yet been made for set wireless lessons. The following broadcasts have been heard today

10·5 — 10·15 news for Schools – Juniors & Seniors

26ᵗʰ. Wireless lessons:- Infants :- Let's join in 11·40 –12.

Juniors :- Stories from World History 2·20 – 2·40

Civilian safety

Stimulus material

'The Protection of Your Home Against Air Raids', Home Office Publication.
'Mr Sensible Says . . .', *Daily Express*, May 1940.
School log book, 1941.

Background

After air raids, many children collected pieces of bomb shrapnel and wreckage from planes. The authorities attempted to discourage this hobby because of the potential danger of finding unexploded bombs, shells and bullets.

On 2 October 1941, a school log book records a visit from Police Constable Phillips who went to remind children of these dangers. Since his talk lasted an hour, it is reasonable to assume that he also talked about general safety issues such as air raid procedure, the blackout, what to do in the event of seeing a parachutist, etc.

Suggested activity

Write a script for the talk given by PC Phillips or design a leaflet to be left with the children to remind them of what they were told.

CONTENTS

(from 'The Protection of Your Home Against Air Raids' – Home Office publication)

Sept. 2nd. A talk was given this afternoon from 2pm - 3pm by P.C. Phillips. of the Battle Constabulary on the dangers of touching strange objects found lying about the countryside.

1941

Mr. Sensible says—stay away from the windows

ONE of the things which Mr. Sensible will emphasise is—*if there's any air activity near your home STAY AWAY FROM THE WINDOWS.*

This means stand or sit where you cannot see out of the window. Then you are out of line of flying splinters.

The importance of this advice has been underlined by the result of expert investigation into the crash of a German bomber at Clacton on April 30.

It has been established that at least half, probably three-quarters, of the 156 injured were cut by flying glass.

It is practically certain, say the experts, that if they had obeyed orders to keep under cover and away from windows few would have been hurt.

Sense from— Mr. Sensible.

(*Daily Express*, May 1940)

News reports

Stimulus material

Newspaper reports from the *Daily Mirror* during the Battle of Britain, August 1940.

Background

Hitler knew that if he were to mount a successful invasion of Great Britain, then he would first have to clear the skies of the Royal Air Force (RAF). In the summer of 1940 he ordered his own air force to bomb planes and aerodromes across south-east England. However, the RAF fighter pilots took to the air and successfully shot down hundreds of German aircraft, sometimes taking off six or seven times a day to turn back the bombers. People in the south-east watched what became known as the 'Battle of Britain' being fought in the skies above their heads.

Suggested activities

Read both newspaper reports of the German attacks and the RAF defence.

What do you notice about the language of both reports?

Can you find examples of the writers using language that would reassure their readers that the battle was being won by the British?

Can you find examples of damage to our forces and civilians being minimised (played down)?

Newspaper reports are supposed to give a balanced view, so why did the editors of the paper allow such biased (one-sided) reporting?

Use one of the reports and, taking some of the details, rewrite it from the German point of view. You will need to give the report a different bias so that readers of the German paper will be reassured that the battle is still going to plan despite some losses.

200 NAZI RAIDERS ARE BEATEN

TWO hundred German planes, crossing the south-east coast in waves which varied from twelve to thirty machines, made repeated attempts to penetrate inland yesterday, but each time they were promptly driven back by British fighters.

The Nazi airmen flew at a great height in an effort to escape the British airmen, but they could not get by—and turned back without having dropped any bombs.

Before they fled the raiders made tip-and-run attacks on barrage balloons.

Now and then ground gunners caught a glimpse of the raiders and " let them have it " with anti-aircraft guns.

When our fighters went into action, the crack of machine-guns was heard, but little could be seen owing to the banks of cloud in which the Germans hid themselves as they roared away.

Toward London

Later it was reported that about a dozen enemy aeroplanes penetrated into a south-east district towards London.

They were travelling at a tremendous height.

British fighters went up and with anti-aircraft fire tackled the enemy. The Germans immediately fled southwards. No bombs were dropped.

Another message said that German bombers crossed the south-east coast yesterday afternoon in isolated groups of three or four apparently unescorted by the usual layers of Messerschmitts.

Their presence was indicated by bursts from our A.A. batteries and they were drive **n**off by our fighters.

Streets Gunned

In the south-western area Nazi airmen machine-gunned a town.

Two planes dived low and wildly gunned the streets. A man was injured by a splinter. He was the only casualty.

One high explosive bomb was dropped and caused a gorse fire.

While people watched the planes at their ruthless work, others took what shelter they could. No one was injured and little damage was done. The A.R.P. service was promptly in action.

The plane dived over the workers in the fields and sprayed them with bullets. They threw themselves flat and escaped.

Some incendiary bombs were dropped. They fell on the common without doing any damage.

A woman said that a German plane swooped low and tried to bomb the farm building, but was not successful.

(*Daily Mirror*, 30 August 1940)

144 DOWN OUT OF 1,000

or

ENNY
aper.

This bus was damaged in the Croydon raid.

(*Daily Mirror*, 16 August 1940)

A HUNDRED AND FORTY-FOUR ENEMY RAIDERS WERE BROUGHT DOWN UP TO MIDNIGHT YESTERDAY.

That was Britain's answer at the end of the day of the greatest air attacks of the war, in which the German "blitz" swept the length of Britain.

Twenty-seven R.A.F. fighters were lost in the mighty defence battles, but eight of the pilots are safe.

For hour after hour through the day, and then into the night, our fighters swept against the huge raiding squadrons.

The German Air Force used more than a thousand bombers and fighters in the attacks.

Croydon Aerodrome, London's airport before the war, was raided last night. "Bombs were dropped on and around the aerodrome," said the Air Ministry later. "Some damage was done, but details are not yet available."

Sirens were sounded in a wide area of Greater London.

Many towns were attacked during the day, and a number of people killed. R.A.F. aerodromes in the south-east and in the north-east were bombed.

Heavy attacks on south-east areas went on into the evening hours. All the time German machines were being shot out of the sky.

Over one coast district R.A.F. fighters and the guns smashed up a three-hour attack by 250 raiders.

Once again there was a spell in which German planes were dropping out of the sky at the rate of one a minute.

14 Dive-Bombers

At another point the destruction of several barrage balloons cost nine raiders. People in yet another district saw eight of a big attacking squadron destroyed.

It was the most gruelling day for the R.A.F. fighters. And their greatest.

Fourteen dive-bombers, protected by fighters, attacked Croydon Aerodrome. High explosive "screamers" and incendiary bombs were dropped.

Some people were killed and a number injured.

The raiders were first seen when they started to dive about three miles from the aerodrome. People in the streets saw them come to a few hundred feet before the bombs were released.

Within a few seconds anti-aircraft guns put up a fierce barrage. R.A.F. fighters swept to the attack. Three of the raiders are believed to have been smashed.

One bomb narrowly missed a gas-works, but houses in an adjoining road were hit.

Main casualties of the raid were caused by a bomb which wrecked a building where men were working.

Hours afterwards rescue workers were still digging in the debris for bodies of the victims.

Not far away a bomb dropped only a few yards from a bus and blew out a 30ft. wide crater.

Passengers were injured by flying glass as all the bus windows were blown out. Part of the engine was

Contd. on Back Page, Col. 2

Contd. on Back Page, Col. 2

Speak like an RAF Officer!

Stimulus material

List of wartime slang expressions, especially those used by RAF Officers.

Background

RAF Officers often used slang expressions and spoke in short sentences. This may have been the result of being trained to communicate by radio.

Suggested activities

Use the table opposite to translate the following monologue by an imaginary RAF Officer:

'What ho old boy! Have you heard about Clement's shaky do? Apparently he was flying his crate over the drink when he met up with bandits.

'The upshot was he caught a bullet in the jacksie and had to ditch.

'He would have bought it if it hadn't been for some fishing chappies who pulled him out of the drink and flung him in a meat wagon in Portsmouth.

'I spoke to him on the blower this morning. He wants all his chums to know he has no intention of pushing up the daisies just yet. He says that he hopes to be driving a new bus as soon as the bandages come off.'

Include some wartime slang in your own sentences. Read them out and ask a friend to translate them for you.

Write some dialogue between two RAF Officers. Act it out and ask someone to stand next to you to translate for your audience.

A

ankle biters – children
AWOL – absent without leave

B

bang on – accurate
bandits – enemy planes
blotto – drunk
blower – telephone
bought it – died
bumph – paperwork
(do a) bunk – escape/leave
bus driver – bomber pilot

C

crate – aeroplane
chums – friends
chappie – man
curtain going up – the action is about to start

D

(have a) dekko – have a look
to ditch (verb) – crash-land into water
the drink – the sea

G

gone for a burton – wrecked
get cracking – to start
get his wings – permission to fly solo

H

Hun – German

I

I say – Wow/good gracious

J

jacksie – bottom/backside

K

keep mum – keep quiet
kite – aeroplane

M

meat wagon – ambulance
miss the show – fail to take part in the action

O

old gal/old boy – affectionate names for friends

P

prang – crash
prune – idiot who takes risks
push off – to go/leave
pushing up the daisies – dead

R

ropey – bad/poor quality

S

(lovely) spread – delicious meal
shaky do – bad experience
spiffing – very good
sardine tin – submarine

T

tiddly – slightly drunk
tear off a strip – tell off
tail-end Charlie – rear gunner
turn off the tap – stop crying

U

US – unusable/broken
under-the-counter goods – stolen goods/ goods sold in contravention of rationing
upshot – the result
Uncle Sam – America

W

wizard – excellent
What ho! – Hello
Wheeze – good time/good idea

Y

Yanks – Americans

Salvage

Stimulus material

Dialogue between Superintendent Salvage and Detector-Inspector Waste.
Photograph: 'Out of the Frying Pan Into the (Spit)fire' (p. 58).
From Section 2: 'The Salvage Song' (The Housewife's Dream) (p. 58) plus Salvage rhymes (p. 59).

Background

The Minister for Aircraft Production, Lord Beaverbrook, made a request: 'Give us your spare pots and pans and we will turn them into Spitfires, Hurricanes and Wellingtons.' The response was tremendous as families believed that they were doing something towards the war effort. Along with saucepans and frying pans came tin baths, tin cans and garden railings.

Good Housekeeping magazine suggested that children form 'Street Squads' to collect salvage and take it along to official collection depots.

Suggested activities

With a partner, read the 'Superintendent Salvage' dialogue.

Note how this script is set out with the Superintendent's words in italics and the Inspector's words in ordinary typescript. Note too how each name is in bold type.

Now write a new script using the same two characters as they visit a house or go from house to house trying to persuade housewives that many of their cooking utensils could be sent for salvage.

You may wish to feature the voices of the housewives who may be a little annoyed or flustered by the over-zealous activities of Superintendent Salvage and Detector-Inspector Waste.

Produce a wartime cartoon for the line 'A Dornier chased by my kettle' or the short rhyme beginning, 'The war is driving Hitler back . . .'

Superintendent Salvage, with Detector-Inspector Waste, take charge for the holidays

The Superintendent: *Now, Inspector, let's have your report.*

The Inspector: Well, sir, everything's mostly according to plan. I have my men in every house and a Sergeant acting directly under each grown-up Salvage Steward.

The Superintendent: *Good. How's the Bone Hunt progressing?*

The Inspector : Things are moving. My house constables check up on every joint that comes to the house and personally superintend plate clearance after each meal. They are also present at each emptying of the stock-pot and take account of all bones given to the dog. These are all reclaimed and put into the Bone Tin. Every other day, the house constable takes the tinful to the street collector's post and adds it to the bone collection.

The Superintendent: *What about fish bones?*

The Inspector: Ah, we don't make the mistake of putting *them* in, but all other little bones, even rabbit bones, are carefully salvaged.

The Superintendent: *Keep going—if every bone in every house is saved the country will have the bones to produce nitro-glycerine to propel hundreds of thousands of shells.*

The Inspector: The Waste-paper Search is going on relentlessly. The instructions are as follows Every day, house constables collect the previous day's newspapers and any finished-with magazines, together with letters that have been answered and all wrappings from parcels

The Superintendent: *String is included?*

The Inspector: Certainly—string is a vital ingredient in paper-making. Once a week old cheques and receipts are collected from the grown-ups and taken to the bank for repulping. No secret leak out this way !

The Superintendent: *What about paid bills?*

The Inspector: They're collected once a week from Mothers' shopping baskets, and odd bus tickets are searched for, too, and the kitchen drawer inspected in case too many paper bags have accumulated.

The Superintendent: *Have you tracked down that case of Pig-swill Poisoning yet?*

The Inspector: Yes, sir ! At No. 4 Home Drive one constable was not alert enough in seeing that NO coffee grounds and rhubarb tops went into the bucket with vegetable trimmings and plate scrapings. He knows the seriousness of this slackness, and won't offend again.

The Superintendent: *Well, carry on, Inspector, and don't forget that the Case of the Elusive Rubber must be tackled next. Not an old hot-water bottle, a rubber boot, a worn-out rubber ring, or an old bicycle tyre must escape.*

The Inspector: Very good, sir. The Squad is on the job !

MOTHERS

Make the children responsible for Salvage Collections. They'll enjoy doing a worthwhile job and they'll probably help to keep you up to the mark yourself.

SALVAGE STEWARDS

The youngsters make good helpers—especially if you appeal to their imagination. The above are suggestions for getting them interested. Organise your Street Squad these holidays, and watch the Salvage pile up

Turn waste into our biggest war weapon.

Every scrap of paper saved, Helps to free all those enslaved.

(from *Good Housekeeping* magazine)

Rationing and the black market

—◄ ⊙ ►—

Stimulus material

Information on rationed goods.
'Do YOU Buy From a Black Market?' (*South London Press*).
Wartime memories of Mrs Allum (below and p. 66).

Background

In an attempt to ensure the even distribution of basic foods, the government introduced a system of rationing. Meat, sugar, butter, cheese and tea could only be purchased if ration coupons were handed in to shopkeepers.

In many places, a 'black market' developed where individuals illegally obtained rationed food and sold it to members of the public at inflated prices.

Some people considered this to be outrageous criminal behaviour, while others were prepared to take part in these deals because they were desperate to provide a sufficient supply of quality food for their families.

Suggested activity

Write a letter to Winston Churchill, the local paper or the police to express your views on whether the black market activities can be justified in any circumstances.

Before the war I had a job making travelling goods, suitcases and things and of course that had to close because people didn't want that kind of thing. And it was let out to a packing case makers by the name of Breed from Aldershot. My father had a friend there and he got me a job making boxes for bombs using hammers and nails. We made hundreds of them. They used to allow us to have the offcuts of the wood for our fires at home because coal was scarce. We used to take a big bag for the wood and sometimes someone would offer us tea or something on the black market. Once I got some sugar on the black market so that was all buried in my bag under the wood. When I got on the bus to go home I was trembling in case anyone asked what was in the bag because it was an offence. You had to pay double for black market things compared with what you normally paid. Some people made a lot of money out of it.

My husband's father had a brother. He lost his arm in the First World War. He used to work where the boats came in. If we saw him coming along, we knew we'd got some butter coming! He used to bring the butter by packing it round himself! We used to say 'Uncle Albert's coming!' – we knew we'd have some butter.

(Wartime memories of Mrs Allum)

DATE	BACON & HAM	SUGAR	BUTTER	COOKING FATS	MEAT	TEA	CHEESE	PRESERVES (MONTH)	POINTS RATION (MONTH)
1940 JAN. 8	4 oz	12 oz	4 oz						
1940 JULY 22	4 oz	8 oz	AND MARGARINE 6 oz	2 oz	1/10	2 oz			
1941 MAY 5	4 oz	8 oz	6 oz	2 oz	1/-	2 oz	1 oz	8 oz	
1941 DEC. 1	4 oz	12 oz	7 oz	3 oz	1/2	2 oz	3 oz	1 LB	16 POINTS
1942 FEB. 23	4 oz	8 oz	6 oz	2 oz	1/2	2 oz	3 oz	1 LB	20 POINTS

MILK AND EGGS:
(PROPORTION ONLY, EXACT QUANTITIES VARYING)

ASSUMED ADULT ENTITLEMENT ➤ 3 PINTS OF MILK A WEEK — 3 EGGS A MONTH

SPECIAL SUPPLIES: MILK –				
EXPECTANT MOTHERS: 7 PINTS	INFANTS: 14 PINTS	CHILDREN: 3½ TO 7 PINTS	INVALIDS: UP TO 14 PINTS	12 EGGS A MONTH FOR CHILDREN AND EXPECTANT MOTHERS

OTHER EXTRAS FOR CHILDREN:	ORANGES	FRUIT JUICE CHILDREN UP TO TWO YEARS	COD LIVER OIL CHILDREN UP TO SIX YEARS

Do YOU Buy From A Black Market ?

" THEFTS of rationed food from the docks and warehouses go on every day. As long as the thieves can find people to buy stolen goods they will go on stealing," said Mr. Frank Powell, Tower Bridge magistrate, on Friday.

Sidney Samuel Evans (49), ganger. 185. Rosebery-avenue. E.C.1. was fined £3 for having in his possession four pounds of tea, suspected stolen, at New Kent-rd.

When stopped by the police. Evans said he had bought the tea for 10s. in the street from a man he did not know.

A police officer said there was a ready sale for rationed foods in the streets in these days and large quantities changed hands every day in this way. People who in the ordinary way would not dream of buying anything they suspected of being stolen did not seem to have any scruples about buying rationed food without coupons.

(Anyone buying rationed food without coupons, or having more than their coupons entitle them to, are " in unlawful possession " of such goods, and therefore open to prosecution.)

(*South London Press*)

Delicious dishes?

Stimulus material

War-time advertisement for Peek Frean's Puddings, recipes from McDougall's *Wartime Cookery Book* and further wartime recipes.

Background

Rationing often made it difficult for people to produce appetising meals. Food companies tried to find new methods of advertising to make their products appeal to consumers. The Peek Frean's advertisement attempts to promote the image of a tasty, easy-to-prepare meal.

Suggested activity

Look at the advertisement for Peek Frean's Puddings. Discuss how effective it is. Imagine that your company has decided to produce one of the wartime recipes in a can. Find a way to advertise the product to make it appear as appealing as possible. You may change the name of the dish but the ingredients must remain the same!

CAN A WARDEN BE A GOOD WIFE?

Mrs. X discovers how!

Save the situation, and the ration coupons, too, with a Mrs. Peek's Pudding! READY MADE for you by the famous house of Peek Frean, from old family recipes. Perfectly sweet, no extra sugar needed.

Mrs Peek's PUDDINGS

6 kinds: Xmas, Light Fruit, Dark Fruit, Date, Ginger, Sultana . . . 1/-

Made by PEEK FREAN & CO. LTD. · MAKERS OF FAMOUS BISCUITS

SHEEP'S HEAD BROTH (2 Meals in One).

1 Sheep's Head and Trotters (dressed). 2 Carrots. 2 Leeks. 2 Onions. 1 Turnip. 1/2 Cabbage. Salt and Pepper. 1/4 lb. Pearl Barley or Rice. Cold Water.

Wash the head and trotters thoroughly, put them into a saucepan, cover with cold water and bring to the boil. Add the rice or barley and cook for one hour. Grate or slice the vegetables, add them and the seasoning and cook for two hours. Lift out the head and reserve for dinner the next day. Serve the broth.

COW HEEL STEW.

1 lb. Cow Heel. 1/2 lb. Carrots. 1/4 lb. Onions. 2 tablespoonfuls Rice. Salt and Pepper. Water. Suet Pastry (see page 19).

Wash the heel and cut into three or four pieces. Put it into a saucepan with the sliced onions, carrots and seasoning. Cover with water, bring to the boil and add the rice. Stir occasionally to prevent the rice sticking, and cook for one hour. Prepare the pastry, roll into a round slightly smaller than the saucepan, and put it on the top of the stew. Replace the lid and boil for twenty to thirty minutes, according to the thickness of the pastry. Lift the pastry on to a plate, cut into four, and put the meat, vegetables and liquor on to a dish, and place the pieces of pastry around.

SHEEP'S HEAD AND PARSLEY SAUCE.

1 Cooked Sheep's Head. 1/2 pint Milk. 1/4 pint Broth. 1 1/2 oz. Margarine. 1 1/2 oz. McDougall's Self-raising Flour. 1 dessertspoonful Chopped Parsley.

Cut the meat from the head into neat slices, chop the brains, skin and slice the tongue.

Melt the margarine, add the flour and cook for a minute, then stir in the liquids by degrees. Bring to the boil, season, add the meat, brains and parsley. Simmer for ten minutes and serve.

PIG'S TROTTERS AND DUMPLINGS.

4 Pig's Trotters. 1/2 lb. Carrots. 1/2 lb. Onions. Salt and Pepper. Cold Water. Chopped Parsley. Dumplings (see page 24).

Wash the trotters, put them into a saucepan, cover with cold water and simmer steadily for two hours. Add the sliced carrots, onion and seasoning and cook for another hour.

Make the dumplings, drop into the boiling liquid and cook, covered, for twenty to thirty minutes according to the size.

Lift the dumplings on to a hot dish, place them around the edge, put the trotters in the middle and arrange the vegetables around. Sprinkle a little chopped parsley over and serve the liquor in a hot jug.

This dish may be cooked in a casserole in the oven if more convenient.

(from McDougall's *Wartime Cookery Book*)

PARSNIP PUDDING

INGREDIENTS

Cooked, cold parsnip
cocoa substitute
bicarbonate of soda
$^1/_2$ pint warm milk
sugar or sweetener

Mix all the ingredients together and place in a greased pie-dish. Bake for $^1/_2$ hour.

BREAD AND CHEESE CUSTARD

INGREDIENTS

Bread and butter (left from tea)
1 cupful grated cheese
1 pint milk
2 eggs
pepper and salt

Grease a pie-dish, cover the bottom with bread and butter, cover with grated cheese, then bread and butter again and more cheese. The last layer should have butter on top. Beat the eggs, add the milk, salt and pepper. Pour into the dish and leave to soak for $^1/_2$ hour. Cover with grated cheese and bake in a moderate oven for about $^1/_2$ hour and serve hot.

DAMPER

(This recipe was published in the press following several queries from readers as to its origin. The paper replied: 'As we remember it, it is a sort of bread made by bushmen in Australia, is quickly made and is very palatable.' Damper was apparently eaten in the Channel Islands at the turn of the century and revived during the Occupation.)

INGREDIENTS

$^1/_2$ self-raising flour
large pinch salt
enough water to mix a dry
*   dough*

LIMPET OMELETTE

2 quarts limpets
1 bay leaf
2 small leaks
1 egg
parsley
salt and pepper

Put the limpets into cold water, bring to the boil, strain and remove shells. Return limpets to the pan and simmer with the bay leaf and a little pepper and salt until quite tender. Strain. Remove the heads and strings and mince the limpets. Chop the leeks and mix them with the limpets, adding parsley. Put a little fat into a frying pan, add the well-beaten egg and then add the limpet and leek mixture and fry till brown.

(Miscellaneous wartime recipes)

Advertising in wartime

◄ ⊙ ►

Stimulus material

Wartime advertisements for items to be bought at chemists.

Background

Many wartime advertisers began to design advertising campaigns for their products which offered relief from the differing health problems that the war posed for people. The rheumatism product 'Kruschen' recognises that too much digging for victory could lead to muscle strain, while 'Phosferine' offers help to people whose nerves are strained or who are feeling run down.

Other products offered quick relief of symptoms in people who were too short of time to look after themselves properly.

Suggested activities

Read the advertisement for 'Kruschen'. Note how the gardener's photograph makes us believe that he gives the product his personal recommendation. We also believe that he will be 'diggin' for victory' with even more enthusiasm now that he is taking 'Kruschen'.

Develop a health product of your own. It could be one that relieves tiredness, nervousness, back pain, foot strain, toothache, earache, colds or flu, headache or something similar.

Think of a name for the product and then think of someone from the Second World War who could recommend your product – a fireman, ARP warden, policeman, Land girl, spitfire pilot, soldier – and write out their recommendation to go with it.

Plan a publicity campaign for the product. Design a newspaper advertisement to persuade people that they need your product. You can imply that it will help them in their war effort. Alternatively, enlist the help of others and script a radio advertisement for different voices. Compose a slogan or an infuriating jingle, the sort that advertisers love because it gets into your head and you can't get rid of it!

Extension activity

In design and technology sessions design a box or tin for your product. Think what you need to put on the label.

Careless talk costs lives

Stimulus material

Various posters reminding the public to be careful about what they say.

Background

These posters formed part of a campaign for National Security. They warned people to be careful when talking aloud in case they unwittingly gave away information to enemies of Britain.

The Ministry of Information produced two-and-a-half million posters for display in offices, shops and public houses. These featured such slogans as 'Careless Talk Costs Lives', ' Be like Dad – Keep Mum!' and 'Keep it under your hat!'

'Think Before you Speak' stickers were also stuck on telephones.

Suggested activities

Produce further slogans to help the 'Careless Talk Costs Lives' campaign.

Take either 'Be like Dad – Keep Mum!' or 'Keep it under your hat!' and produce an eye-catching poster that reminds people to think before they speak. Where would be a good place to display the poster?

If you've news of our munitions
KEEP IT DARK
Ships or planes or troop positions
KEEP IT DARK
Lives are lost through conversation
Here's a tip for the duration
When you've private information
KEEP IT DARK!

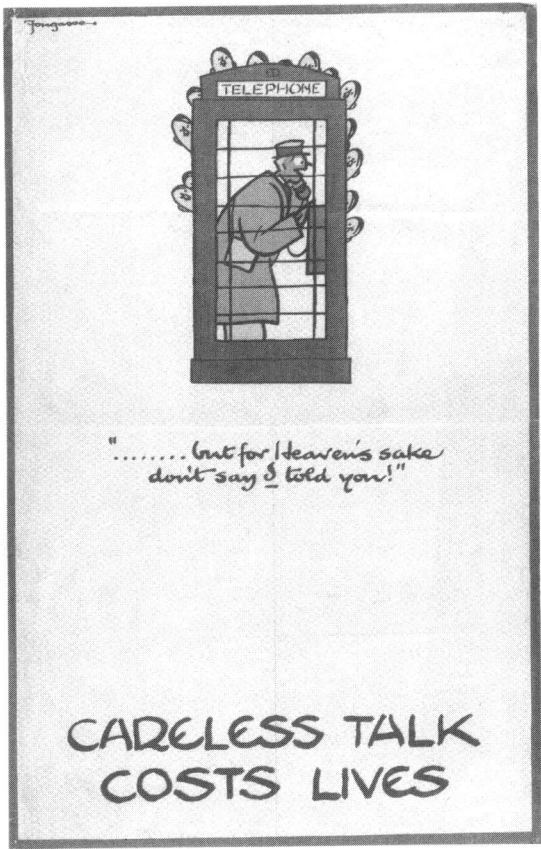

Make do and mend

➤ ⊙ ◀

Stimulus material

Exchange and Mart advertisements.
Newspaper article 'MAKE MUCH of your SHOES'.

Background

As the war progressed, many goods were in short supply as more and more factories converted to producing weapons and ammunition. 'Make-do-and-Mend' classes and radio programmes were full of good advice – how to make clothes last longer, how to patch carpets or make toys out of cotton reels.

In the Channel Islands, which were occupied by German troops from 1940 onwards, there was a great shortage of clothing and footwear. People bartered (swapped) among themselves or put advertisements in the local newspapers.

Suggested activities

Read the *Exchange and Mart* advertisements. What problems might result from such exchanges? The paper would probably have published a list of rules and regulations concerning such bartering. Can you work out what they might have been?

Produce an advertisement of your own to fit such a column.

What might you have been in need of in 1941?

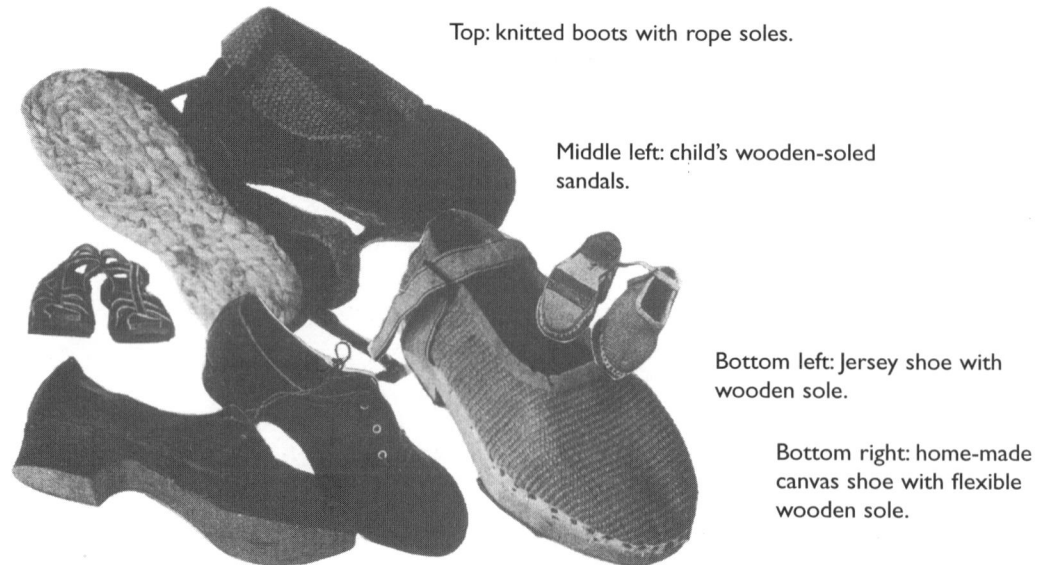

Top: knitted boots with rope soles.

Middle left: child's wooden-soled sandals.

Bottom left: Jersey shoe with wooden sole.

Bottom right: home-made canvas shoe with flexible wooden sole.

(German Occupation Museum, Guernsey)

"MAKE MUCH of your SHOES..."

MANY of us have been rather careless about shoes, but now we've got to make much of them. THEY MUST LAST . . . .

Here are six of the main causes of premature wearing-out of footwear:

(1) DRYING SHOES near a stove or radiator. The application of HEAT to shoes, especially if they are wet, destroys the fibrous nature of the soles and often transforms the leather into a hard glue-like mass.

(2) TOASTING YOUR TOES near a fire. Partial burning or scorching of shoes can bring about rapid wear, without any marked evidence of burning. This condition is usually shown in two ways: (a) The sole is a good thickness in some parts but wears to wafer thinness in nearby parts; (b) The uppers of the shoes are affected by the scorching and are more liable to perish and crack across the vamps.

(3) CONSTITUTIONAL EFFECTS. The uppers of shoes will deteriorate before their time if the wearer has any constitutional tendency towards rheumatism or gout. Uric acid and urinary matter deteriorate leather and uric poison is often exuded in foot perspiration.

you do not sponge it off the shoes immediately.

(6) OIL, GREASE or LIGHT will soon perish any kind of rubber footwear.

THEREFORE

as you want your footwear to LAST as long as possible, will you please read and note the following:—

If you have more than one pair of shoes, never wear the same pair two days following. Remove your shoes when you reach home at night; put them on hollow trees, sponge them with an almost dry sponge and allow them to dry slowly—away from the fire. The following evening, clean the shoes with a good WAX polish (such as P.Q.). Heavy work-boots should be washed and dressed daily with P.Q. DUBBIN, which penetrates the stout leather better than a WAX polish. (Remember that Dubbin should be well rubbed into the leather, with the hand, and that you cannot shine the shoe afterwards.)

When you sit by your fireside, do wear slippers and save your shoes.

Go through your wardrobe

Make-do and Mend

Doctor Carrot and Potato Pete

Stimulus material

Government posters of Doctor Carrot and Potato Pete.
Newspaper column – Carroty George.

Background

Posters such as these reminded children how important it was to eat plenty of these vegetables. Carrots contain Vitamin A, and one of the Doctor's messages was that extra Vitamin A would help everyone see better in the blackout. (Not really true, as huge amounts would need to be eaten for any real difference to be noticeable!)

Eating potatoes saved bread, prevented tiredness and its Vitamin C helped keep away infection. Potato soup would be nourishing on cold winter nights. It could be warming for fire watchers on duty, and was taken into air raid shelters as a meal for everyone.

As fresh fruit wasn't always available, people were also encouraged to eat lots of green vegetables as alternatives.

Suggested activities

Find out about the healthy qualities of other vegetable such as parsnips, turnips, swedes and beetroot.

Use this information to devise a cartoon character who could promote the vegetable – Professor Parsnip, Bertie Beetroot, Tracey Turnip for example.

Design an advertising campaign to increase the public's awareness of the benefits to be gained from eating such vegetables. Can you make up a rhyme to go with it:

> Potato Pete, Potato Pete,
> See him coming down the street,
> Shouting his good things to eat,
> 'Get your hot potatoes
> from Potato Pete'.

DOCTOR CARROT the Children's best friend

Carroty George

He's a great favourite in the kitchen, our Carroty George. He has a hundred and one ways of making himself agreeable. Given a chance he'll enter into your pots and pans with real relish. Even if you reduce him to dice he won't be cut up ; and he takes frying, steaming, stewing or boiling, in perfectly good part. He plays the leading part in

Club Carrots

Scrub and grate 6 large carrots and mix with a teaspoonful of finely shredded white heart of cabbage. Make a dressing of 1 small teacupful thick unflavoured custard, 1 tablespoon salad oil, 1 teaspoon vinegar, ½ teaspoon each mustard, pepper, and salt, and 1 tablespoon finely chopped pickles. Toast 4 thick slices of bread on each side, then slit open to make large pockets. Spread the insides of these pockets with margarine, and stuff with the filling. Serve at once. **A first-rate supper dish.**

I make a good Soup !

Says 'POTATO PETE'

Issued by the Ministry of Food.
Printed for H.M. Stationery Office by
Stafford & Co., Ltd., Netherfield, Nottm. 51-8938

The Squander Bug

Stimulus material

Poster – 'Don't take the Squander Bug when you go shopping'.
Hints on wartime spending and saving.

Background

The Squander Bug appeared in 1943. The government warned people that the Squander Bug caused that 'fatal itch to buy for buying's sake – the symptom of shopper's disease'. This meant that you should only spend money on the things that you really need. Other money should be saved by buying special savings certificates. This money could then help the war effort as the government could use all money that wasn't needed immediately to fight the war.

The 'Here are three ships' poster reminded everyone that if ships didn't need to bring in so many unnecessary goods there would be more space for essential items such as foodstuffs and munitions (weapons and ammunition).

Suggested activity

Write a conversation between two Squander Bugs. The first has persuaded a boy to waste his money on something he doesn't really need, while the second has persuaded the boy's sister to do the same. The bugs will be delighted with their work.

You could draw the bugs in a series of cartoon pictures, with the conversation as speech bubbles.

Hey diddle diddle,
Don't finger or fiddle,
Those notes are a full week's pay.
The Squander Bug wants you to
fritter the lot,
Keep on saving and drive him away.

BUY 3% DEFENCE BONDS

BECAUSE:

The interest is paid regularly half-yearly.

The Bonds are repayable at par ten years after date of purchase plus premium of £1 per cent.

Defence Bonds can be bought in multiples of £5 for cash or with 6d., 2 6 or 5/- Savings Stamps collected in easy stages.

They are on sale at Banks and at most Post Offices.

Here are three ships

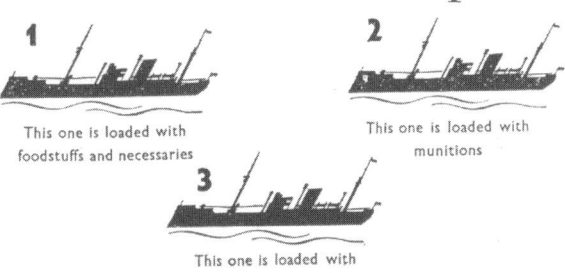

1 This one is loaded with foodstuffs and necessaries

2 This one is loaded with munitions

3 This one is loaded with unnecessary goods

By limiting your purchases of the goods con ained in Ship No. 3, you leave more cargo space for the goods we need to win the war. Spend carefully then—buy what you must—but avoid spending on unnecessary things, particularly goods which come from abroad.

Result: (1) *You increase the shipping avail-able for essentials.*

(2) *You have more money to invest in National Savings Certificates and the New Defence Bonds.*

Women at war

⏤ ◉ ▶

Stimulus material

Items from government campaigns to recruit women into the factories.
Salute to the war-workers from Hoover.

Background

At the beginning of the war, women volunteered to work on the land and in the factories, often doing work that was previously carried out by men. After April 1941 women could be directed to work 'for the national interest'. Many women found themselves making weapons and bombs, building ships, fighter planes and gun mountings. Many learnt riveting and welding.

Emotional appeals were made to women in magazines and on advertising hoardings. 'Are you equal to *two* **German** women?' is an example of this sort of 'propaganda' (information that persuades people to support the government's wishes).

Suggested activities

Although women now did the same jobs as men, they still usually earned only half as much in wages. Write a letter to the Ministry of Labour (Employment) outlining your work as a woman in a bomb-making factory. Explain how hard you work, how you work a 60-hour week and how dangerous the work is. Complain to the minister about how unfair it is to be paid only half the wages that a man would get.

Read the two contrasting reports about working in factories in Section 2 (p. 63). Which is more convincing?

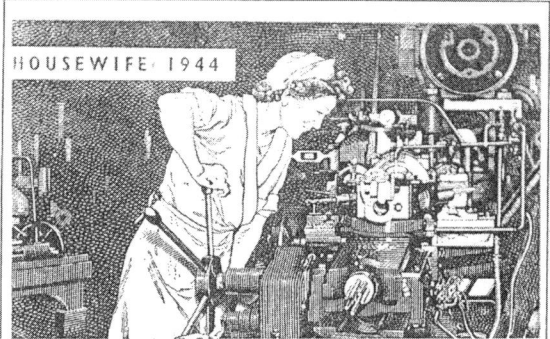

The Hand that held the Hoover works the Lathe!

With no glamour of uniform, with all the burdens and responsibilities of running a home, thousands of housewives in 1944 are war-workers too. They are doing a double job. They get no medals for it. But if ever women deserved especial honour, these do. So to all war-workers who also tackle shopping queues, cooking, cleaning, mending and the hundred and one other household jobs

Salute! FROM HOOVER

Hoover users know best what improvements they would like in the post-war Hoover. Suggestions are welcome.

BY APPOINTMENT TO H.M. KING GEORGE VI AND H.M. QUEEN MARY
HOOVER LIMITED. PERIVALE. GREENFORD. MIDDLESEX

WOMEN OF BRITAIN
COME INTO THE FACTORIES
ASK AT ANY EMPLOYMENT EXCHANGE FOR ADVICE AND FULL DETAILS

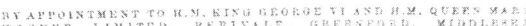

Are you equal to two German women ?

Two of Them to Every One of You

'Your opposite number in Germany has spent her year in a labour camp. Her limbs are strong, her stride is firm, and her spirit is uplifted by a perverted idealism. She labours willingly, passionately, indefatigably, in the shipbuilding yards and the heavier industries, for one end – the glorious defeat of Britain and the triumph of Nazism. For the men over military age are not enough, two million enslaved Poles are not enough, the Italian arsenals are not enough, to feed the German war machine… if Britain is to be humbled and crushed. So the German women pour out of the kitchens and into the factories… Two of them to every one of you.'

Wartime Christmas

Stimulus material

Christmas cards sent home from troops stationed abroad.
'One Man's War' – Section 2 (p. 78).

Background

Christmas was always a sad time for those separated from families and homes. Soldiers abroad sent back greetings cards which were read by the censor to check that no one gave away details of exactly where the troops were.

In Britain, Christmas was very much an 'austerity' celebration. Toys were in short supply as toy factories had been taken over for weapon production. Presents were often home-made or picked up at jumble sales. Quite often stockings simply contained an orange, a sweet and a tiny toy.

Suggested activities

Can you improve on the design of cards given to the troops? Keep them black and white and think carefully about an appropriate illustration and wording.

What would be written in the card? Read 'One Man's War' (p. 78) and put yourself in the place of the soldier who is spending Christmas 1942 in North Africa away from family and friends. What sort of message would he be sending home? Check that the card would pass the censor.

(The censor's job was to read all cards and letters sent from the army unit to relatives and friends. If the censor thought that any sentences gave too much away he would strike them through with a black pencil so that they were unable to be read.)

Sender's Address : ....

Christmas 1943

Greetings from 18 Casualty Clearing Station

ON THIS DAY WE PAUSE
AND YOU ARE WITH US

CHRISTMAS GREETINGS FROM
THE MEDITERRANEAN

from Harry X.

Occupied Britain

$$\blacktriangleleft \!\!-\!\!\! -\!\!\! \odot\!\!\! -\!\!\! \blacktriangleright$$

Stimulus material

'Orders of the Commandant of the German Forces on Occupation of the Island of Jersey.'

Background

The Channel Islands were captured by the German army in June 1940 and occupied by German troops until May 1945.

What happened on the main islands of Jersey and Guernsey gives us an idea of what would have happened throughout Britain had Hitler's invasion plans proved successful.

Once they had occupied the islands, German commanders issued a series of orders restricting the activities of the islanders and warning against anyone causing trouble.

Suggested activities

Radios were taken away and anyone caught with one could be fined or imprisoned. Despite this, many islanders found ingenious places for concealing radios and carried on listening to the news from London.

Imagine that you are a Channel Islander with a radio to hide. Discuss where you would hide it to make absolutely certain that any search of your house would fail to find it.

As the war went on, food became scarce in the islands. Some food was stolen from the Germans and in an account of such an incident on Guernsey, Molly Bihet writes about being caught by a German soldier stealing potatoes:

> . . . my, did I run! But with his long legs and massive big boots he eventually caught me up and gave me such a kick! My pride was really hurt and I ran home crying and rubbing my bottom.

Imagine that this incident is followed up by the German authorities who visit Molly's house and speak to her parents. Write the conversation between Molly's parents, Molly and two German soldiers who have come to warn Molly's parents that she must behave in future.

Produce the conversation as a playscript and act it out.

Orders of the Commandant of the German Forces in Occupation of the Island of Jersey

1. All inhabitants must be indoors by 11 p.m. and must not leave their homes before 5 a.m.

2. We will respect the population in Jersey; but, should anyone attempt to cause the least trouble, serious measures will be taken.

3. All orders given by the Military authority are to be strictly obeyed.

4. All spirits must be locked up immediately, and no spirits may be supplied, obtained or consumed henceforth. This prohibition does not apply to stocks in private houses.

5. No person shall enter the Aerodrome at St. Peter.

6. All Rifles, Airguns, Revolvers, Daggers, Sporting Guns, and all other Weapons whatsoever, except Souvenirs, must, together with all Ammunition, be delivered at the Town Arsenal by 12 Noon to-morrow, July 3rd.

7. All British Sailors, Airmen and Soldiers on Leave, including Officers, in this Island must report at The Commandant's Office, Town Hall, at 10 a.m. to-morrow, July 3rd.

8. No Boat or Vessel of any description, including any Fishing Boat, shall leave The Harbours or any other place where the same is moored, without an Order from the Military Authority, to be obtained at The Commandant's Office, Town Hall. All Boats arriving in Jersey, must remain in Harbour until permitted by the Military to leave.

   The crews will remain on board. The Master will report to the Harbourmaster, St. Helier, and will obey his instructions.

9. The Sale of Motor Spirit is Prohibited, except for use on Essential Services, such as Doctors' Vehicles, the Delivery of Foodstuffs, and Sanitary Services where such vehicles are in possession of a permit from the Military Authority to obtain supplies.

   The use of Cars for private purposes is forbidden.

10. The Black-out Regulations already in force must be obeyed as before.

11. Banks and Shops will be open as before.

12. In order to conform with Central European Time all watches and clocks must be advanced one Hour at 11 p.m. TO-NIGHT.

13. It is forbidden to Listen to any Wireless Transmitting Stations, except German German Controlled Stations.

14. The Raising of Prices of Commodities is Forbidden.

(Signed)

THE GERMAN COMMANDANT OF THE ISLAND OF JERSEY.

The Welsh Great Escape

Stimulus material

Daily Express, Monday 12 March 1945. 'The Escape from Island Farm, Bridgend, Wales.

Background

During the war, captured forces personnel were imprisoned in 'prisoner of war' camps. They were known as POWs.

On 12 March 1945 British newspapers reported the escape of approximately 70 German prisoners of war from a camp in Bridgend. The Germans had escaped through a tunnel under the perimeter fence. For several days they had been singing loudly to disguise the sound of tunnelling. Twenty-eight of the men were caught quickly but the others were able to avoid immediate recapture. Embarrassingly, four prison guards helped some of the Germans to start a car and drive it away before they realised who they were! The car belonged to the local doctor.

Many of the Germans attempted to hide in the local woods until nightfall and people from the town joined in the search for them. Some of the Germans were spotted by local children who knew the best places for hide and seek games.

The following day it was reported that a young woman had told her father of a small wood in a hollow where she had played as a child. Acting on her information, the young woman's father had gone to the wood and found a group of the escaped prisoners. Police arrested these men soon afterwards.

The four men who had stolen the doctor's car eventually ran out of petrol and were re-captured. It is said that when they found out that the car belonged to a doctor they apologised and offered to pay for the petrol! In the end, all of the Germans were recaptured and returned to the prison.

Suggested activities

Imagine that you were one of the children involved in searching for the prisoners or one of the prisoners who escaped from the camp.

Produce a storyboard that shows the escape from the prison camp, the hunt for the prisoners and their eventual recapture.

Write a diary entry recounting your experiences or write the story in the first person.

DAILY EXPRESS

Blackout 7.28 pm to 6.50 am   MONDAY MARCH 12 1945   Moon rises 7.3 am sets 4.36 pm

Planes hunting 42 escaped Nazis

Secret tunnel break-out

Express Staff Reporter: Bridgend (Glam.), Sunday

SPOTTER planes flew over the Vale of Glamorgan this evening while troops, Home Guards and police, all armed with tommy guns, searched the woods, fields and ditches for 42 German prisoners of war.

Seventy made a mass escape through a secret tunnel from a camp at Bridgend early this morning.

Sixteen were caught soon after the break, and 12 more were recaptured this evening.

While the hunt for the remaining 42 still goes on, the police warned people in the district to lock their homes securely to prevent the fugitives getting food and civilian clothes.

Car and lorry owners were ordered to immobilise all vehicles as the Germans may try to steal them during the night.

Four of the 42, it is believed managed to steal a doctor's car in Bridgend and drive it to Newnham-on-Severn, where it ran out of petrol.

The four men were seen running towards the nearby Forest of Dean, and the alarm was given.

Under the wire

Within a few minutes reconnaissance planes were dipping over the forest while troops, police and civilians joined the search. Home Guards and Special Constables were also called out.

The Germans still at large include 11 Luftwaffe men and several naval officers. The remainder are army men.

The tunnel through which the escape was made was dug under three barbed-wire fences to an open field. One hour before dawn today the Germans made the break-out and scattered in small parties as the guards raised the alarm.

One German is reported to have been shot but not fatally.

It was a rowdy camp and cat-calling and singing have disturbed residents near for some time. It was under cover of this rowdyism that the prisoners completed their plans.

Several hundred prisoners occupy the camp. They include SS men and paratroopers all described as tough devil-may-care youngsters and fanatical Nazis.

News Chronicle

No. 30,933   MONDAY, MARCH 12, 1945   ONE PENNY

70 Nazi prisoners escape

Home Guards and planes in search

SEVENTY German prisoners of war escaped from a camp at Bridgend (Glam.) in the early hours yesterday.

At night 36 were still at large; 34 had been recaptured during the day at various places in the neighbourhood.

There was some shooting, and one prisoner was slightly wounded.

Four stole a car and got into Gloucestershire, where planes were used in the search.

Hundreds of the Home Guard living in Bridgend, which lies about midway between Cardiff and Swansea, at once volunteered to help in the search.

Warning in churches

Regular soldiers, police, Civil Defence workers and farmers were also out. At chapels and churches in the district morning service was interrupted to read police warnings.

VE Day and VE Day celebrations

Stimulus material

School log book 1945.

Background

Among the entries relating to head inspections and the late arrival of the canteen van, are two small entries that indicate the end of the war!

• Victory in Europe, marked by a holiday on 8 and 9 May 1945.

• Victory in Japan, marked by a holiday on 15 and 16 August 1945.

These must have been far more exciting events than the log book suggests. Many parties and celebrations were held immediately after the announcements of the end of hostilities. The end of the war must have been a very difficult time for people who had lost loved ones during the conflict.

Suggested activities

You may be able to find someone who remembers taking part in celebrations at the end of the war. Perhaps you could prepare an interview with them. Start by writing some questions beginning with

• Who . . . ?
• What . . . ?
• When . . . ?
• Where . . . ?
• Why . . . ?
• How . . . ?

(These types of questions result in detailed answers.)

Design a newspaper advertisement to give details of the celebrations that you would have planned in your area. Be sure to provide appropriate activities for all age groups, including the young and elderly. You will need to give details of the time and place for these festivities.

Write imaginary diary entries for people who have witnessed the festivities. You might include a child's diary, the diary of someone who has lost someone in the war, the diary of someone who knows their family is safe.

March 23. Dr Sawyer attended this morning for immunization.

" 28 School breaks up to-day for the Easter holidays.

April 10th School reopened today.

The Seniors left Guestling School today. They proceed to Rye Senior School on Thursday April 12th.

April 16th The School Nurse attended to inspect heads this afternoon

May 8th.9th School closed for two days in celebration of

Victory in Europe

May 11th Dr Sawyer attended for immunization

" 14th Canteen Van arrived at 12.55. so the afternoon session could not begin till 1.30.

15th afternoon session was again deferred till 1.30 owing to the Canteen Van arriving at 1.5.

23rd School closed today for the Whitsun holiday.

- 28th School reopened today.

July 5th School closed today for the General Election.

" 6th Dr. More visited the school this afternoon to examine the special cases.

" :3 Dr. Sawyer attended this morning for immunization.

August 2nd. Miss Dyke P.T organiser visited the school & saw the P.T.

" 3rd. School closed until Wednesday. August 8th.

- 8th. School re-opened this morning.

August 15.16 School closed for two days. V.J.

" 17th School closes today for the summer holidays

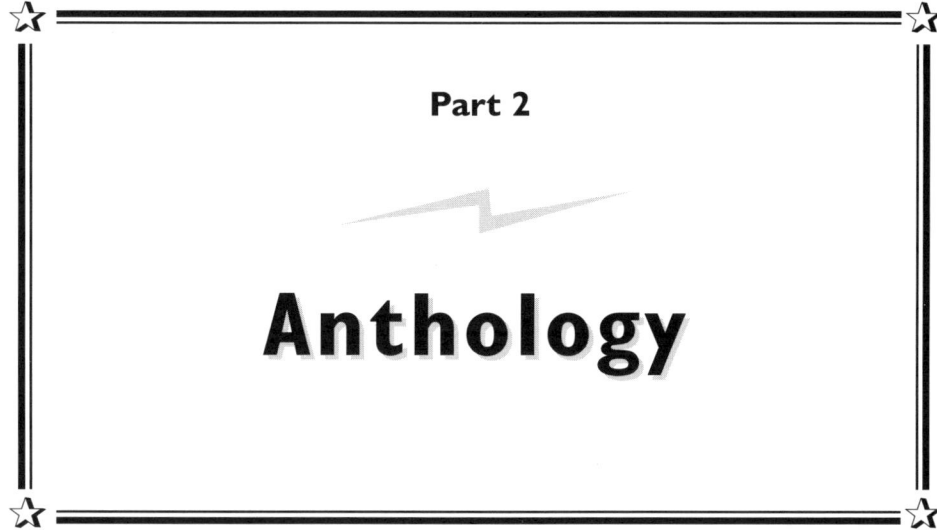

Part 2

Anthology

The day war broke out

Neville Chamberlain's speech on 3 September 1939:

'I am speaking to you from the Cabinet Room at 10 Downing Street.

This morning the British Ambassador in Berlin handed the German government a final note stating that unless we heard from them by 11 o'clock that they were prepared at once to withdraw their troops from Poland, a state of war would exist between us.

I have to tell you now that no such undertaking has been received, and that consequently this country is at war with Germany.

[...]

Now may God bless you all. May He defend the right. It is the evil things that we shall be fighting against: brute force, bad faith, injustice, oppression and persecution. And against them I am certain that right will prevail.'

Evacuation of children from the Channel Islands

Children should take with them:

- Gas mask.

- Two ration books (current and new one).

In addition to clothes being worn – which should include an overcoat or mackintosh –

Girls:
One vest or combination, one pair of knickers, one bodice, one petticoat, two pairs of stockings, handkerchiefs, slip, blouse, cardigan.

Boys:
One vest, one shirt with collar, one pair of pants, one pullover or jersey, one pair of knickers, handkerchiefs, two pairs of socks/stockings.

Additional for all:
Night attire, comb, towel, soap, facecloth, toothbrush, and if possible, boots, shoes and plimsolls.

Rations for the journey:
Sandwiches (egg or cheese), packet of nuts and seedless raisins, dry biscuits (with little packets of cheese), barley sugar (rather than chocolate), apple, orange.

(*Guernsey Evening Press*, Wednesday 19 June 1940)

The end of evacuation 1939–40

I began to get bored – here we were at war and nothing was happening.
The standard of eating in the country was lower than I was used to at home.
Mum and Dad visited me at weekends bringing food parcels; the thought of
returning home with them was very provoking. In London there were
hundreds of barrage balloons, shelters were being built, sandbags were
everywhere. The pace was what I was missing, as well as my home.
My twelfth birthday was spent in West Peckham, and the following Sunday,
heartily homesick, I asked my parents to take me back with them.

London was, for me, like a return from exile. My pet cat met me at the gate,
the neighbours welcomed me and the sun shone. Even my brother didn't
seem to find me so objectionable.

There were no schools open, but the local vicar arranged a class in his
house, using local retired people with some teaching experience to help out.
I joined this class which at least kept us off the streets. We learnt odd
subjects such as Esperanto and Monopoly, all very enjoyable!

(from *Children of the Blitz: Memories of Wartime Childhood*, ed. Robert Westall (Viking 1985))

From an advert for wool

There's more that goes to win a war
Than tanks and planes and guns!
Than men prepared to do their best
To overthrow the Huns.

The Home Front too must play its part
And you can do YOUR bit
To help our gallant fighting lads
By starting now – to KNIT!

You cannot knit too many things
To keep out wet and cold;
Like mittens, helmets, socks and scarves
GO TO IT – young and old!

Salvage Song
(or, The Housewife's Dream)

My saucepans have all been surrendered,
The teapot is gone from the hob,
The colander's leaving the cabbage
For a very much different job.
So now, when I hear on the wireless
Of Hurricanes showing their mettle,
I see, in a vision before me,
A Dornier chased by my kettle.

(Elsie Cawser)

Salvage rhymes

Because of the pail, the
    scraps were saved,
Because of the scraps, the
    pigs were saved,
Because of the pigs, the
    rations were saved,
Because of the rations, the
    ships were saved,
Because of the ships, the
    island was saved,
Because of the island, the
    Empire was saved,
And all because of a
    housewife's pail.

The war is driving Hitler back
But there's one way to win it.
Just give your salvage men the sack
And see there's plenty in it.

Dearly beloved brethren,
It is not a sin,
To peel potatoes and to throw away the skin.
The skin feeds the pigs
And the pigs feed us.
Dearly beloved brethren is that not enough?

I've Finished My Black-out (The Song of a Triumphant Housewife)

I've finished my Black-out!
> There's paint on the carpet and glue on my hair
> There's a saw in the bathroom and spills on the stair,
> And a drawing pin lost in the seat of a chair,
>> But I've finished my Black-out.

The bedrooms are draped with funereal black
Except for the little one facing the back,
And that we have had to nail up with a sack,
>> But I've finished my Black-out!

> Oh, I've finished my Black-Out!
Policeman and warders may peer and may pry,
And enemy planes may look down from the sky,
But they won't see a pin-prick however they try,
>> For I've finished my Black-Out!

(Anonymous)

Dig for Victory

Dig! Dig! Dig! And your muscles will grow big,
Keep on pushing the spade!
Don't mind the worms,
Just ignore their squirms,
And when your back aches laugh with glee
And keep on diggin'
Till we give our foes a wiggin'
Dig! Dig! Dig! to victory.

(Popular wartime song)

A song sung by the Women's Land Army (Land Girls)

Back to the land, we must all lend a hand,
To the farms and the fields we must go,
There's a job to be done,
Though we can't fire a gun,
We can still do our bit with the hoe;
When your muscles are strong,
You will soon get along,
And you'll think that the country life's grand;
We're all needed now,
We must all speed the plough,
So come with us — back to the land.

Women working in factories

Working in factories is not fun. To be shut in for hours on end without even a window to see daylight was grim. The noise was terrific and at night when you shut your eyes to sleep all the noise would start again in your head.

Night shifts were the worst . . . The work was very often monotonous. I think boredom was our worst enemy.

Going to work in a factory during the war was a wonderful experience. For the first time, I had some degree of freedom from my parents' control; I had money of my own to do with as I liked; and I was being given responsibilities and treated like an adult. I made lots of new friends at work – young women like myself who were having their first taste of freedom.

We felt good about ourselves, and although there were terrible things going on all around us, the war years were the happiest times of our lives.

War rhymes

(These rhymes were recited by children for skipping or chanting.)

When the war is over,
Hitler will be dead,
He hopes to go to Heaven
With his halo on his head.
But the Lord says NO
YOU'LL HAVE TO GO BELOW
THERE'S ONLY ROOM FOR CHURCHILL
SO CHEERY CHEERY OH!

Underneath the churchyard, six feet deep,
There lies Hitler fast asleep,
All the little mice come and tickle his feet,
'Neath the churchyard, six feet deep.

Who's that knocking at the window?
Who's that knocking at the door?
If it's Hitler, let him in
And we'll sit him on a pin,
And we won't see old Hitler any more.

(Anonymous)

Song of the pilots in the Second World War

When you're seven miles up in the heavens
    And that's a heck of a lonely spot,
And it's 50 degrees below zero,
    Which isn't exactly hot,
When you're frozen as blue as your Spitfire,
    And you're scared as Mosquito pink,
When you're thousands of miles from nowhere,
    And there's nothing below but the drink –
It's then you will see the gremlins,
    Green and gamboge and gold,
Male and female and neuter,
    Gremlins both young and old.

White ones'll wiggle your wing-tips,
    Male ones'll muddle your maps,
Green ones'll guzzle your glycol,
    Females will flutter your flaps,
Pink ones will perch on your perspex,
    And dance pirouettes on your prop.
There's one spherical middle-aged gremlin
    Who spins on your stick like a top.
They'll freeze up your camera shutters,
    They'll bite through your aileron wires,
They'll cause your whole tail to flutter,
    They'll insert toasting forks in your tyres.

(Anonymous)

Second World War memories

(Written from a transcript of conversations with Mrs Allum.)

The lead-up to war

I was born in Morning Lane, in Hackney. By the time that war broke out, I was married. I got married in '37 and I went to live in Balls Pond Road in Dalston. War broke out on the Sunday morning in September '39. People knew it was going to happen because of Chamberlain. And they had invaded Poland hadn't they? Everybody was expecting it but they were a bit apprehensive. We got it on the radio at eleven o'clock in the morning – that's when it happened.

The first air raids

We had air raid shelters in the garden, corrugated ones they were but it was quite quiet for a while. My husband was called up in April '40 and he had to do three months footbashing and one thing and the other. His first weekend leave was when they set the Surrey Docks alight. It was quite a fine day. It was on the Saturday afternoon. Everybody was out of their houses and you could see the smoke. We could see and hear the planes coming over. It was quite shocking. That's when it more or less started.

In the shelters

Most of the bombing was after dark. We had to have blackout curtains. You mustn't show a chink of light and there were no street lights on. If you went out you took a torch with you but you held it in the palm of your hand so the light couldn't be seen from above. We were prepared for it and we had to go into the Anderson shelter every night. We took the dog with us and the cat but there wasn't much you could do in there really. We took blankets with us because it was cold. We had a candle alight and torches, but you had to be so careful. You were on tenterhooks all the time in case they started bombing. Every night we were out in the shelter because we couldn't take a chance. Even if you'd been in the shelter all night, you got up and went to work as usual in the morning. People who didn't want to go into the shelters went down the Underground. They used to sleep on the platforms because it was deep under ground. They took all their worldly goods with them – even their beds. They used to make tea and take their supper down there. You had to go down loads of stairs in those days. You may have heard of the Bethnal Green incident. Someone fell on their way into the shelter and everyone went over on top of them. There was ever such a lot of people killed.

Unexploded bomb

I'm not quite sure how long into the war it happened, but the road I lived in – Hawthorne Street it was, a cul-de-sac with about 25 houses in it near the main road – Kingsbury Road. They dropped a land mine. We heard this thing coming. When we got up in the morning and we came out of the shelter, the Police came and said we've got to get out because in Kingsbury Road this land mine had landed but it hadn't gone off. I always kept a case packed with anything I valued so we had to get out quickly and I picked up my case and I put my best shoes on. I thought, 'I won't leave them behind.' But coming down the stairs I broke my heel off! The policeman said, 'You've got to go to the school', but my husband said, 'That's not far enough away from where it is.' Anyway he had a sister who lived a fair distance away. So that's where we went. It was about seven o'clock in the morning and when we got to his sister's, she said, 'What's the trouble?' and he told her and she said we could stay there because she had a big house. It wasn't far from my parents, so I said, 'I think I'll go home.' I walked home and my father answered the door and he said, 'What are you doing here?' and I said, 'I've been bombed out!' Anyway, it didn't go off so they had to get a naval officer but he got killed when he was trying to defuse it and the damage was really extensive. There was broken glass everywhere and when we went to see what damage there was to our house, they wouldn't allow us in. The Council went in and sorted out what was left and they stored it for us. That was our first experience of it really.

War work and the black market

Before the war I had a job making travelling goods, suitcases and things, and of course that had to close because people didn't want that kind of thing. And it was let out to a packing-case makers by the name of Breed from Aldershot. My father had a friend there and he got me a job making boxes for bombs using hammers and nails. We made hundreds of them. They used to allow us to have the offcuts of the wood for our fires at home because coal was scarce. We used to take a big bag for the wood and sometimes someone would offer us tea or something on the black market. Once I got some sugar on the black market so that was all buried in my bag under the wood. When I got on the bus to go home I was trembling in case anyone asked what was in the bag because it was an offence. You had to pay double for black market things compared with what you normally paid. Some people made a lot of money out of it. I worked in Bermondsey and it was a horrible journey. I used to leave home about seven in the morning and never got home until late at night because I had to have two buses. It was ever so cold, this place where I worked, with concrete floors and steel benches. The heating was combustion stoves and they put sawdust in them. They wouldn't take married women in the Services. If you got married once you were in, that was all right. My two sisters went into the Air Force but I had to go on war work and I didn't want to go to Birmingham on ammunitions because if you didn't have another job you had to go. My husband said that I ought to go back with him to Nottingham but I didn't go – not for some time. I did that job until I got pregnant and then of course I left it. By this time I was living in some rooms next door to my in-laws. We used to get bombing pretty regular – every night – and everything was rationed. I can't remember the actual amount but I think I had about two ounces of butter per week. The flour was rationed, cheese and the meat – you got liver and offal sometimes. If the rumour went round that there was some in the shops, everybody used to go and queue. My husband's father had a brother. He lost his arm in the First World War. He used to work where the boats came in. If we saw him coming along, we knew we'd got some butter coming! He used to bring the butter by packing it round himself! We used to say, 'Uncle Albert's coming!' We knew we'd have some butter.

Evacuees

All the children in the area were evacuated soon after the declaration of war. My husband's youngest brother went – he was about twelve at the time. They hadn't got a suitcase for him so I lent him one. People pulled together much more than they do now. It was a frightening experience for them. They all had their gas masks – you had to carry that gas mask wherever you went – to work with you, bed with you. I don't think he was gone more than about a month but he didn't like it so he came back.

More bombing

They set the City of London alight one night. I think it was on a Sunday night. You never saw anything like it. There were hoses everywhere. Buses were driving over them, there was devastation everywhere. It was really awful, smoke everywhere. A lot of people got killed. Eventually I went to Nottingham with my husband because things were getting bad. He found me a lodging and the government encouraged you to go. They gave you about eight shillings a week towards the lodging. He told me that he would meet me at Nottingham Station. I got there on time but there was no sign of him. I hung about until about five o'clock in the afternoon but he never turned up. I wondered if they'd sent him somewhere and he hadn't had a chance to tell me, but then a lady told me there were two stations in Nottingham – he was at one and I was at the other! I made friends with the lady who told me about the stations. Her husband was a bar manager and he asked me if I'd like to work evenings in the bar. I got a job making khaki trousers in the day and I worked in the bar in the evening. We had rations for clothes. It was hard to buy them so we had to do things like turn an old coat into a skirt. But I managed to get a black dress made. The bed in my room in Nottingham was facing the window and we had a bomb. People kept banging on my door saying, 'Come on, get out!' All of a sudden the window was blown in, so I had to get out quickly. The door was ripped off the bookcase, but amazingly none of my tea set on the shelf was touched. It was the first bombing they'd had up there but of course I knew what to expect! It was the headquarters of Boots that they bombed. They got in a real panic. Next door was an off-licence. The windows were all smashed and there were people running through the glass on the pavement with no shoes on. The landlady had a friend who lived in the middle of town so she wanted to go into town to see how she was. I told her to pack a bag and take a warm coat in case we couldn't come back. We took what we could and went. Where she'd been living had caught the blast and she was in bed upstairs with the walls and roof gone. She had to stay up there until they sent for her to be rescued!

Doodlebugs

By the time my son was born in 1944, the doodlebugs had started. Sometimes I had to go out and leave the baby with my in-laws. If the sirens went, I used to run all the way home! When the noise of the engine stopped, you knew the bomb was coming down! By this time I was back in London. My husband was allowed 24 hours leave to come and see me and the baby. He met me at King's Cross. As we stepped out of the station, the sirens went. We went to my Mum's in Hackney because they lived in a basement and he thought we'd be safer there. They weren't expecting us so there were no preparations for the baby and he had to sleep in a drawer! Sometimes we took shelter in the cupboard under the stairs.

One day I saw a doodlebug fly over and I was so scared for my baby I jumped down twelve stairs all in one leap just to get to him quickly. If you were out in the High Street, they had brick-built shelters on the pavement and you had to dive into one of those. Once the Americans came into the war we got a bit more food. They brought us over Spam and that kind of thing. My sister got engaged to an American and he used to bring a big bag of oranges for the baby! We couldn't get anything like that. We had to make do with concentrated orange juice, but rationing carried on.

The end of the war

On the day the war was over, everybody was going to have a drink. We had a big pub on the corner near my mother- and father-in-laws. He was a sorter in the post office and when he got home at ten o'clock at night, he used to meet my mother-in-law in the pub. That's where we all went, although my husband was away. I had my baby in the pram and he cried because he could see everyone with a glass of beer and he wanted one! Nobody went to bed that night. People went mad! Although it was very sad for people who had lost someone. We were very lucky not to lose anyone. My brother-in-law was at Dunkirk. He got the last boat out. He swam out from the shore because they wouldn't take any more – they could only take a certain number. He was covered in blood and he climbed up the side of the boat and they took him. My youngest sister went over to Dunkirk because she was a nurse and she helped to bring the injured back. They took the injured back to Cardiff. My husband wasn't released from the Army until 1946.

Families reunited

My son was about eight months old before my husband saw him again. When he did manage to get to see us, the baby had a cold and my husband was so worried about him he didn't want to go back. The Red Caps came and took him away the next morning about six o'clock. After that he didn't see him again until he was about eighteen months old. But I had a photo of my husband and I used to show it to my son and tell him, 'That's your Daddy.' When my husband finally did come home my son was with me. When I opened the door he hid behind my back. He was frightened of this man with all his kit. He didn't realise that it was his Dad! Of course my husband was upset about that. Things took a long time to settle down. People would go mad nowadays if they couldn't go to the shops and buy the food and clothes they wanted. Of course if you weren't born then, all this is like a story. People don't realise how well off they are now.

The Channel Islands: Guernsey

THE STAR

Notice

It must now be known to a good many local inhabitants that some 8 persons recently left this island in a boat with a view to reaching England.

As the direct result, drastic control of boats has been instituted by the German Authorities, resulting in fishermen in the northern and western parts of our island being unable to follow their vocation and depriving the population of a very large proportion of the fish obtainable.

Any further such departures or attempts thereat can only result in further restrictions. In other words, any persons who manage to get away do so at the expense of those left behind. In these circumstances, to get away is a crime against the local people, quite apart from the fact that the German Authorities will deal very severely with people who are caught making the attempt.

In the event of a repetition of any such incident, there is a grave possibility, by way of reprisal, that the male population of this island will be evacuated to France.

A. J. Sherwill

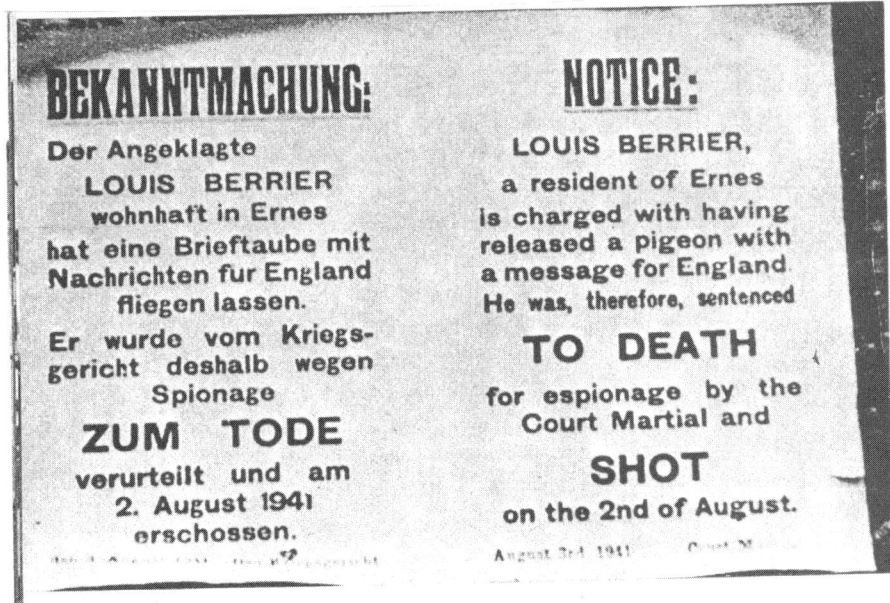

BEKANNTMACHUNG:

Der Angeklagte
LOUIS BERRIER
wohnhaft in Ernes
hat eine Brieftaube mit
Nachrichten für England
fliegen lassen.
Er wurde vom Kriegsgericht deshalb wegen
Spionage
ZUM TODE
verurteilt und am
2. August 1941
erschossen.

NOTICE:

LOUIS BERRIER,
a resident of Ernes
is charged with having
released a pigeon with
a message for England.
He was, therefore, sentenced
TO DEATH
for espionage by the
Court Martial and
SHOT
on the 2nd of August.

August 3rd 1941   Court M...

The Channel Islands:
A letter to Father Christmas

Vauvert School,
10 December 1940

Dear Father Christmas,

It is perhaps too much to expect you to visit us this year. The sky over Guernsey is rather dangerous but if you could arrange to come in a Junkers 52 I suppose you would get here safely. I'm hoping you will come; we have just had the chimney swept specially for you so that your white fur will not get dirty, and my pillow-case will be in its usual place at the foot of the bed so that you will be able to leave what you have brought without having to fumble much in the blackout.

Could you bring me some chocolate? I have not had any for three months. I would adore a good hunk of Dutch cheese also, and about two dozen eggs would be lovely if you could get them across without breaking them. Even one egg would be very acceptable. Christmas dinner will not be its usual self without a leg of pork so if you could slip one into my pillow-case I would be very thankful. I know all this is rather a lot to ask you but you usually manage to provide our requirements. Oh – and don't forget the fruit – oranges, dates and nuts. Lemons are not so important.

I wouldn't mind a few toys but the townspeople are kindly taking on your job this year as regarding toys, and if you are only going to bring playthings, perhaps you had better not risk the trip. Anyway, I hope you have a safe journey, if you do decide to make the attempt, and that you will not find it necessary to camouflage your reindeer.

Yours,

Betty Boswell

(Taken from *A Child's War* by Molly Bihet (1985))

The Channel Islands: Wartime recipes

Wartime recipes from the Channel Islands

Marrow and sugar beet jam

Cut large marrows and cook until tender, then strain off all water.

Mash marrow and add sugar or sweetener to taste.

Pour in a half-pound pot of sugar beet syrup and add one tablespoon of carrageen powder.

Boil for a few minutes. Put in jars.

Parsnip pudding

Take some cooked cold parsnip.

Mash with cocoa, add bicarbonate of soda.

Warm a half-pint or more of milk.

Sweeten with sugar or sweetener, then mix all ingredients together and bake in the oven for half an hour.

Substitute for tea

Gather young stinging nettles. Wash and dry in the sun. When dry, crumble up and use as tea. It may be boiled to draw out the flavour.

Put on an old pair of gloves for picking the nettles and use a toasting fork to pick out of the water as they remain prickly.

This used once a day makes a good beverage and tonic.

Interview: Mrs Ivy Green, Ramsgate

During the Blitz in World War II, the safest places for people to escape the bombing were deep underground shelters where no bombs could penetrate. Londoners sheltered from the bombs in the Tube stations, sleeping on the platforms. People in Nottingham made use of a system of natural caves beneath the town.

Ramsgate in Kent is one of only two towns in Europe to have purpose-built deep shelters. (The other is Barcelona which withstood some of the heaviest bombing of the Spanish Civil War.) Work started on Ramsgate's tunnels in the spring of 1939. A central tunnel, which had previously brought the railway to Ramsgate seafront, was expanded and linked to many smaller passages. The chalk on which Ramsgate is built was very easy to cut and needed no propping. Work was completed just before war broke out and the system stretched for three miles at an average depth of 67 feet. There were 22 entrances and the whole population of Ramsgate could shelter in safety.

I interviewed Mrs Ivy Green, who was eleven years old when war began and spent much of the first three years of the war living in these tunnels.

When did you first go down the tunnels?
The first time I went down the tunnels was on 24 August 1940 after a very heavy air raid when the gas works blew up. There were only about six children in Ramsgate at the time, all the rest having been evacuated, but my father worked at the gas works and he wasn't allowed to move. So we all stayed. My mum said that if a bomb got one of us it would get the family.

Can you describe the tunnels?
There was a large central tunnel and a system of smaller ones that led into it from entrances around the town. The main tunnel was actually used by a miniature railway before the war began, and those of us who were sheltering there would sleep in deckchairs or blankets on either side of the tracks. As time went on, huts were constructed from black sacking, we were number 71. The huts were different sizes, larger ones with double bunks for families and smaller areas for couples.

The bunks were really comfortable. My sister was in the top one, my younger sister and I in the bottom one and mum and dad in a bed that they'd taken down there.

So you began to think of the tunnels as home?
My mother put curtains round the chalky walls and across the door to make it private and homely. We had lino on the floor. We had the cat and the budgie down there, and a radio. The mums were always sweeping and polishing. We cooked on Primus stoves – the collection of different cooking smells was amazing, as were the meals that mothers prepared. My dad used to come to the tunnels straight from work and that was home.

Could you hear anything of what was going on at the surface?
If there was a raid up top we'd hear a plonk and the place would shake. If the bomb was a big 1,000-pounder and it landed above where we were, the lights would go out and soot used to blow down from the roof.

What were the tunnel entrances like?
Entrances to the tunnels were mostly wide and well lit. We went down about ten or twelve flights of steps to the passages. The seafront end of the main tunnel was open to begin with but it was eventually blocked up to prevent the Germans from gaining access if they ever invaded.

As a child, how did you adapt to life under ground?
We made our own amusements. We'd go up the passages and carve our names in the chalk. We did sewing and took comics down. For an 'afternoon out' we'd walk though the tunnels to a canteen that was established near Dumpton Station. There were no schools in operation at that time so my father taught us what little he could.

Can you recall any special events?
My sister had a party in the tunnels for her eighth birthday. We rummaged together and everyone gave a little bit of their ration. At Christmas too there were parties for the children – everything 'make do and mend', jellies were made from gelatine and all toys had to be hand made. People got married from the tunnels. One couple suffered an air raid in the middle of their wedding service. They had to go back down the tunnels and then finish the service when the raid was over.

Were there amusing incidents?

One in particular. The only transport in the tunnels was a plate-layer's trolley which was formerly used by workmen repairing broken plates that joined lines together on the miniature railways. In the night someone would push this trolley along the lines and then let it go. We wondered what was coming. It made a dreadful creaking and cranking. Nobody could stop it until it got to the end of the line. Soldiers on leave who were sheltering in the tunnels were great jokers and would often be responsible for the trolley's late-night run.

What was the mood of people in the tunnels?

It was a very happy atmosphere. We all looked out for each other. We shared happy news and we shared each other's sorrows – if anyone lost their home or a member of their family. There was no bickering, we all got on with each other. You had to do that or you'd go under. We were safe down there though, we knew nothing could penetrate. We'd hold dances and concert parties to keep our spirits up.

When did you leave the tunnels?

From August 1940 till late 1941 or early 1942, we'd often go for two or three weeks without seeing daylight. We couldn't go up top because the warden would send us back down as the air raids were too bad. Eventually it was decided that we shouldn't be living down there completely and we had to come up during the day. But if there was a raid we got back down there really quickly.

(Brian Moses)

Friend or Foe
by Michael Morpurgo

In *Friend or Foe* two evacuees, David and Tucky, are convinced that a German plane crash-landed near their new home, but despite an extensive search of the surrounding hills by the authorities, nothing is discovered. The two boys search the hills themselves but disaster strikes when David falls into a stream and is close to drowning. He is rescued by one of the two Germans from the crashed aircraft. When David recovers, his rescuer makes a request:

'My friend is not well,' the German said. 'He cannot move much and he is cold. I need food – food and blankets. The nights are cold here and he coughs. Will you help us please?'

'Help you!' David was almost shouting. He pulled himself to his feet, gathering the greatcoat around him. 'Help you? After what you've done? You come here bombing and killing and you want us to help you!'

'It is a war,' he replied sadly. 'In war people die – on both sides.'

'Why don't you give yourself up?' Tucky said. 'You can't escape, not if your friend can't move. And there are soldiers out looking for you, you know. We told them about your plane.'

The German threw more wood on the fire. 'Perhaps you are right,' he said, 'but we must try. We need time to recover. Two days ago we have finished the emergency food. We have nothing left – just water from the river. This is the first fire I have dared to light. We must keep warm, and we must have food. Then we will escape over the moor to the sea and find a boat.'

'What about the soldiers?' said Tucky.

'They did not find us last time. It is a big place to search, this moor.'

'And what if we tell them where you are?' David said, as defiantly as he could.

'Then we shall be caught, my young friend. I cannot move my friend any more now, and I cannot leave him. We are in your hands.' And he turned away and walked back to his friend on the other side of the fire.

'What do we do?' Tucky whispered. 'We've got to help him, haven't we? He saved your life, Davey, pushed all the water out of you and he was risking a lot to light that fire for you. You owe him, Davey. We both do.'

'He's a German, isn't he? He's probably bombed over London . . .'

'But he saved your life Davey. He needn't have done it. He could have let you drown.'

One man's war
7389233 Pte Harry Moses

Spring 1941: Joined army and did basic training in Aldershot and Leighton Buzzard.

June 1941: Joined 18CCS (Casualty Clearing Station) a unit of the RAMC (Royal Army Medical Corps) and in August journeyed to Kilmarnock in Scotland.

September 1941: Harvesting at North Cairn Farm, Stranraer.

October 1941–February 1942: Working in the operating theatre at Buchannan Castle, Drymen.

1942: Stationed at Stirling Castle for five months where he showed visitors round the castle in his time off duty.

1942: Three weeks spent on the Isle of Wight practising invasion exercises.

October 1942: Sailed on the Greek ship *Nea Hellis* and arrived in Algiers, North Africa, 22 November. The harbour was raided a few hours after they disembarked.

November 1942: After five days embarked for Bone, then Addi Abdullah where he spent Christmas amidst the hills and mud under canvas.

February 1943: Moved to Thibar and then to Sedjenane and Tabarka

Bitter fighting in Sedjenane

NIGHT – and over the darkened plain
The guns roll back from Sedjenane
Not in defeat, or dark despair
For their throats have chorused a battle air
All day to the skies over Sedjenane
Back in the red Tunisian mud
Red with the flow of our English blood.
Men are lying, some dead, some dying,
They fell in the fight for Sedjenane.
We were there too, in that mouth of Hell
'Neath the whispering rush of German shell
At the unending crash where mortars fell,

Fell on the road from Sedjenane.
We saw men come in twos and threes
With bleeding hands and bloody knees.
We saw men come from that place of death
With the Reaper's song in their laboured breath,
They fought so well for Sedjenane.
So we left the town with its silent dead,
Came back with the guns from that place of dread.
The world was told and 'twas truly said,
It was bitter fighting at SEDJENANE.

(Author unknown)

20 October 1943: After a stay of almost eleven months, left North Africa for Italy.

Newspaper report from the local paper in Harry's home town:
With the North African campaign successfully finished, Pte Harry Moses RAMC
has found time to write to some of his local friends. In one letter he says that the
end came far more quietly than had been anticipated.

'I wonder how you at home took the news when you first heard it,' he writes.
'For our part we were all very excited towards the finish, especially when we
watched a convoy of several hundred prisoners go by our camp. There were, of
course, men from all the services, some arrogant, others more subdued and as
usual with servicemen, quite a lot singing. On the whole, the impression we gained
was that they were thankful it was finished.'
. . .
Writing to his mother, Harry says he found the Victory March very inspiring.
'Watching it,' he continues, 'I couldn't help feeling proud that we had helped in
some small way to bring the North African campaign to its successful conclusion.
We saw Generals Giraud and Eisenhower, and the cheering from the tremendous
crowd was deafening. Britain, America and France were all well represented and
the greatest sight was the tanks driving through three abreast and the bombers and
Spitfires coming over in waves.
'Since then, we have bathed in the Mediterranean and one would think the spot
where we swim was a nudist camp. There are hundreds of us in our birthday suits,
either swimming or basking in the sun . . .'

24 October 1943: Landed Taranto in Italy, attached to 19 CCS RAMC unit.

28 January 1944: Left to join 4th Canadian CCS at Vasto and then on to Orvieto.

April/May: Operated on wounded from huge battle to capture the monastery at Monte Cassino.

1 August: Joined 70 General Hospital at Pompeii.

2 September: Moved to Florence, operated in a villa situated in the Old Town.

10 February 1945: Joined 71st General Hospital in Loreto.

April 1945: A week's leave in Rome, sightseeing and along with many others seeing the Pope in the Vatican City.

22 May 1945: In Venice, then on to Udine and through the Alps in an army lorry into Austria.

September 1945: Travelled from Austria through to Calais and across the Channel to England.

8 February 1946: Demobbed at Aldershot (officially left the Army).

Notes on anthology selections

The day war broke out

Older people in their seventies or eighties may still remember where they were or what they were doing when war was declared. If possible, children could interview someone they know to discover how people felt at that time. Make a collection of these responses. What were people's main worries at the time? Were they optimistic or pessimistic? Can they remember the preparations that were being made for war in the places where they lived? (See also: Second World War Memories: Mrs Allum, p. 66).

Evacuation of children from the Channel Islands

Children could write an account of an evacuee's journey from home to new home. Try to focus on how children would have felt – nervous, apprehensive, frightened. How would these feelings have shown themselves? What about saying goodbye to parents and climbing on board trains? How quickly would time pass on the journey? And at journey's end, what sort of welcome would there be?

(Read accounts of evacuation in *Carrie's War* by Nina Bawden, *Friend or Foe* by Michael Morpurgo, and *Fireweed* by Jill Paton Walsh.)

The end of evacuation

Older people again may have personal memories of evacuation and some may be prepared to visit and answer children's questions.

From an advert for wool

How effective would such an advert be, and how useful were the results? There were often problems with distribution of such items, resulting in huge stockpiles!

Salvage Song and Salvage rhymes

Children may enjoy producing wartime cartoons for the line 'A Dornier chased by my kettle' or the short rhyme beginning, 'The war is driving Hitler back . . .'

I've Finished My Black-out

Britain was blacked out by night from 1 September 1939 until 17 September 1944 for fear of air raids. Between those dates it was illegal to let any light shine from a building in case German bombers saw lights below and would know where to drop their bombs. Preparing to put up the blackout each night took valuable time and was considered a nuisance by many until bombs began to fall in the summer of 1940. This anonymous piece is great for recitation.

Dig for Victory and A song sung by the Women's Land Army

People were asked to grow vegetables wherever they could. Lawns and flower beds, playing fields and golf courses were dug up and planted as part of the government's 'Dig for Victory' campaign.

Children might like to try to compose a second verse to the 'Dig for Victory' song.

The Land Girls worked on farms, taking the place of men who were in the services. To begin with, many farmers were sceptical about whether young women could take the place of men, but after a while this was often replaced by grudging respect for women who were able to pull manure carts or catch rats in great numbers.

Children could compose a letter to *The Times* from a farmer who admits that he doubted whether Land Girls could be of any use, and outlining the many varied and often unpleasant tasks that they showed they could do. All letters to *The Times* begin, 'Sir . . .'

Women working in factories
Read the two contrasting reports about working in factories.

Can children produce pen portraits of the women behind these reports?

What would they look like? Are they married, married with a family or single? Are their husbands at home or fighting overseas somewhere? Where do they live?

War rhymes
Children may be able to find other examples.

Song of the pilots in the Second World War
Ask children to explain what the poem is all about.

RAF pilots were a superstitious lot. Quite often they had certain routines prior to take-off that they needed to stick to. They had lucky mascots to take with them on every flight, or a lucky scarf, pendant, photograph, etc.

If something went wrong with the plane, it was the gremlins again and, as the poem says, there were gremlins for everything.

Second World War memories: Mrs Allum
Children could prepare a news report regarding the unexploded bomb. Where did it happen, what time, who was involved? They could feature interviews with Mr and Mrs Allum and the policeman.

Children could also research some of the areas that Mrs Allum mentions – how were unexploded bombs dealt with, how extensive was the Blitz in London, how much of a menace were the doodlebugs?

The Channel Islands
Children should be aware that Hitler did put some troops on British soil when Germany occupied the Channel Islands. They should discover the whereabouts of the islands and realise that Hitler considered their capture as a stepping stone to a full invasion of Britain.

Anyone disobeying the German laws would be treated harshly, as can be seen in the notice from the *Star* newspaper and in the proclamation announcing the death of an islander for espionage.

'A letter to Father Christmas' offers the child's perspective from the first occupation Christmas, while the recipes will sound pretty unpalatable to most children.

(*Wartime Cookbook: Food and Recipes from the Second World War* by Anne and Brian Moses, published by Hodder Wayland, is a source of further recipes.)

Interview: Mrs Ivy Green, Ramsgate
Suggest that children use the information given here and write a detailed account of a night in the shelters. Other material may be added from reading around the subject of shelters and shelter life. Alternatively this could be written up as a page in a diary.

Friend or Foe

This story looks at a situation where it is necessary for the characters to re-evaluate their views.

Aside from the moral dilemmas posed by the concept of war itself, there are marvellous opportunities here to explore the 'grey areas' between right and wrong. The children should stand back from their own preferences and list the reasons why both courses of action might be adopted – helping the enemy or turning him over to the authorities.

Don't just read the extract, the whole book is a great read.

One man's war

This is a précis of my father's wartime scrapbooks. It details his time as a soldier in the Royal Army Medical Corps from when he joined the army in 1941 until his leaving in 1946.

Children may like to follow his progress on a map (or maps) and to find out information about some of the places where he was stationed. (Brian Moses)